Without bias : a guidebook for nondiscriminatory communication / International Association of Business Communicators. 2nd ed. New York : Wiley, 1982.
200 p. : ill.
ISBN 0-471-08561-8 : 10.95

1. Communication in personnel management. 2. Discrimination in employment.

Without Bias:

A Guidebook for Nondiscriminatory Communication

International Association of
Business Communicators

Second Edition

John Wiley & Sons
New York
Chichester
Brisbane
Toronto
Singapore

175 YEARS OF PUBLISHING 1807 1982

Library of Congress Cataloging in Publication Data:

Main entry under title:

Without bias.

Includes bibliographical references and index
1. Communication in personnel management.
2. Discrimination in employment. I. International Association of Business Communicators.
HF5549.5.C6W57 1982 658.4'5 81-16457
ISBN 0-471-08561-8 AACR2

Printed in the United States of America

10 9 8 7 6 5 4 3 2 1

Preface

Communication provides the legs for bias, carrying it from person to person, from generation to generation. Eventually, however, communication will be the way to end discrimination.

Without Bias: A Guidebook for Nondiscriminatory Communication attempts to create awareness of bias in communication and to offer alternatives, without sermonizing.

The success of our first edition (distributed to more than 70,000 people by the publisher, the International Association of Business Communicators) provided the impetus for this revision. It incorporates new and updated information throughout and presents additional chapters, including one on age discrimination—an indication of the increased concern about bias against older people and children.

As *Public Relations Review* said of the first edition, "*Without Bias* doesn't promote a forced neutrality." Instead, it offers sensible solutions, making all readers, viewers, and listeners comfortable, ". . . without sacrificing some of them on the altar of traditional English usage."

What this book presents is common sense. A "firefighter" even *sounds* more useful than a "fireman." "Grandfatherly" can conjure up a false image of all older people in an era of 65-year-old joggers. The "disabled" accountant may not be "handicapped" at all. Extolling Mr. Simon's substantive accomplishments and indicating that Ann's contribution is decorative deprive an audience of useful information—and certainly diminish Ann.

Without Bias is designed for all "communicators" (whatever their titles) in business, government, education, nonprofit organizations, the public media, and elsewhere who are in positions to influence others. It is especially appropriate for those communicators who have official responsibility for explaining an organization's policies and establishing the tenor of its attitudes.

John N. Bailey, ABC, Executive Director
International Association of Business Communicators

Acknowledgments

In addition to chapter authors, IABC gratefully acknowledges the assistance of Judy E. Pickens, ABC, who coordinated the work of the various authors, coauthored one of the chapters, and edited this second edition.

IABC also thanks the following communicators for their advice:

William A. Cradle, Second Vice President, Chase Manhattan Bank, New York.

P. G. Green, ABC, Manager of Public Information, Canada Safety Council, Ottawa.

Carolyn Johnson, Ph.D., Professor of Journalism, California State University, Fullerton.

Susan Nichols, Public Information Director, The American Cancer Society, Los Angeles Coastal Cities Unit.

C. Glenn Pearce, Consulting Editor in business and organizational communication, John Wiley & Sons, and Associate Professor, School of Business, Virginia Commonwealth University, Richmond.

Irene Piraino Prince, former Research Director, IABC, and now Director of Public Relations for the Lankanau Hospital, Philadelphia.

Paul Sanchez, Director of Communications, Hay Associates, Dallas.

Contents

Without Bias:

A Guidebook for Nondiscriminatory Communication

PART 1

Avoiding Specific Types of Bias

Chapter 1

Regardless of Race: Toward Communication Free of Racial and Ethnic Bias

Chapter 2

Regardless of Sex: Toward Communication Free of Sexual Bias

Chapter 3

Regardless of Age: Toward Communication Sensitive to Older People and Children

Chapter 4

Regardless of Disability: Toward Communication Sensitive to Ability

Chapter 1

Regardless of Race: Toward Communication Free of Racial and Ethnic Bias

by Linda Cook Roberts

The reality of global communities can no longer be considered as approaching. It is here.

More and more countries are becoming multicultural and multilingual. Groups of various heritages are challenging the dominance of Western European influence on daily life in the United States and Canada.

Discrimination based on race, color, and national origin has been with us for centuries. It remains with us now, despite these trends and a claim to being an enlightened society. Our language—with its power to reinforce bias and shape thought—is still stubbornly preserving that "Old World" culture as the standard against which all other groups are judged.

The role of the communicator in our modern

world, then, is to examine that language and select alternatives that recognize a broadening racial and ethnic culture. This chapter presents guidelines in response to that objective.

Stereotypes

A kind of modern folklore has developed around stereotypes of various racial and ethnic groups. So powerful are these images that personal knowledge of friends and public figures may not change them. The fiery Spaniard, hearty German, inscrutable Asian, conservative Briton, and exuberant Italian are just a few examples. Less complimentary are the cold Dane, sleepy Mexican, and miserly Scot.

Be aware of words, images, and situations that suggest that all or most members of a racial or ethnic group are the same.

Stereotypes may lead to assumptions that are unsupportable and offensive. They cloud the fact that all attributes may be found in all groups and individuals. For instance, a communicator may unconsciously assume that all Black or Spanish-surnamed employees or community residents are "poor" or "deprived" when, actually, many are well off and highly educated.[1]

To test for stereotypes, identify with one of the following groups and experience how these words and phrases apply to you and to family or friends.[2]

---

[1]Capitalization of "Black" is now commonly done and accepted, comparable with capitalization of Asian, Spanish, and so forth. However, lowercase is also common and accepted, especially by public media (see Chapter 10). The former style has been selected for this book. See the accompanying discussion on choice of "Spanish-surnamed."

[2]Based on an exercise of the Council on Interracial Books for Children, "How Children's Books Distort the Asian-American Image," *Bulletin*, VII, Nos. 2 and 3 (1976), 5.

Keep them in mind when writing and editing.

ANGLO-SAXON

Aloof
Arrogant
Biased against other groups
Cold
Condescending
Conservative
Controlled
Educated
Egotistical
Enslaving
Even-featured
Fair
Industrious
Law-abiding
Muscular
Pious
Poised
Prim
Proper
Rational
Reactionary
Sanctimonious
Selfish
Slender
Snobbish
Snout-nosed
Soft-spoken
Stuffy
Superior
Weathered

MEDITERRANEAN/JEWISH, ITALIAN, GREEK

Argumentative
Artistic
Blue-collar
Clannish
Criminal
Cultured
Dark
Greedy
Gregarious
Hot-tempered
Intense
Lazy
Male-dominant
Manipulative
Menial
Oriented to trades/shopkeeping
Overripe
Passionate
Philosophical
Pushy
Religious
Smart
Squat
Stocky

Superstitious
Swarthy
Unethical in business
Unmotivated
Untrustworthy
Voluptuous

ASIAN

Artistic
Clannish
Cunning
Delicate
Dexterous
Docile
Evil
Exotic
Expert in martial arts/technology
Imitating
Industrious
Inscrutable
Menial
Myopic
Mystical
Passive
Philosophical
Quick
Reserved
Sagacious
Serene
Short
Shy
Sinister
Sly
Smiling
Stocky
Stolid
Submissive
Subservient

BLACK

Aggressive
Angry
Athletic
Blue-collar
Childlike
Clowning
Dangerous
Dependent on society
Deprived
Dirty
Flashy
Grinning
Happy-go-lucky
Hostile
Hustling
Irresponsible (men)
Lazy
Lithe
Militant
Poor

Powerful
Rhythmic
Shuffling
Soulful
Strong (women)
Sullen
Super-sexually endowed
Swindling
Tall
Ungrateful
Unmotivated
Untrustworthy
Violent
Wary

SPANISH-SURNAMED

Blue-collar
Boisterous
Clannish
Colorful
Crafty
Deceptive
Fiery
Greasy
Heavy
Hot-blooded
Hot-tempered
Humble
Lazy
Macho (men)
Menial
Nonplussed
Passionate
Poor
Religious
Servile
Short
Skilled at crafts
Sleepy
Squalid
Stocky
Subservient
Uneducated
Unintelligent
Volatile
Voluptuous

NATIVE NORTH AMERICAN

Alcoholic
Artistic
Backward
Clannish
Courageous
Dignified
Heathen
Reserved
Savage
Silent
Skilled at crafts
Impenetrable
Pagan
Proud

Stoic	Thin
Strong	Uncivilized
Tall	Warlike

These descriptions spell out the stereotypes behind errors that communicators sometimes make. For example, the writer who describes Mexican children as "well-dressed" may unconsciously be portraying an exception to a mental image of a "poor" or "unkempt" Mexican. Similarly, reference to an "even-tempered Greek" implies that such demeanor is not the norm.

Avoid qualifiers that reinforce racial and ethnic stereotypes.

A qualifier is added information that suggests an exception to the rule.[3] For example, an account of a company event read, "The intelligent Black students were guests as part of an orientation program." Under what circumstances would you write, "The intelligent white students . . ."?

To determine whether or not a qualifier has been used, try this test: Imagine the sentence with "white" in place of "Black" or substitute an Anglo-Saxon surname for a Spanish or Asian one. Bias is subtle. The more deeply it has been assimilated, the more difficult it is to uncover.

DOES THIS SENTENCE . . .	. . . CONTAIN THIS STEREOTYPE?
A well-groomed Black student, John Jones works as a part-time clerk.	Blacks are poorly groomed.

[3]Simon Podair, "How Bigotry Builds Through Language," *Racism and the English Language*, ed. by Robert B. Moore (New York: Racism and Sexism Resource Center for Educators, 1976), p. 13.

Bob Herendez, an exceptionally energetic and conscientious worker	Spanish-surnamed people are lazy, unmotivated.
The articulate Black professor	Blacks lack intelligence, verbal skills.
No retiring, quiet job for her. Betty Wong has chosen a dynamic career as supervisor of	Asians are shy, docile (also female nonassertive stereotype).
Jose Rodriguez, a steady and even-tempered worker	Spanish-surnamed people are volatile, unpredictable.

Identify by race or ethnic origin only when relevant.

Few situations require such identification. For example, announcing the appointment of a company's first Black executive vice president is trite. It is simply no longer news to point out the race of an incumbent in a senior-level position (or any position, for that matter), regardless of whether or not the appointment is a groundbreaker.

Similarly, if an article or television news item mentions a well-known public figure, ask whether or not that person really needs to be identified by race or ethnic origin. To do so may indicate a white reference point. Certainly, some communications justifiably include the subject's race or ethnic origin. For instance, a story that refers to Cesar Chavez, organizer of predominantly Mexican farm laborers, might mention his Spanish heritage. But consider:

IF THIS IDENTIFICATION IS INAPPROPRIATE	. . . IS THIS PHRASING ANY DIFFERENT?
Jerry Brown, noted white California governor	Julian Bond, noted Black Georgia legislator . . . .

Byron White, Supreme Court justice and one of eight whites on the high court . . . .

Thurgood Marshall, Supreme Court justice and the only Black on the high court . . . .

Questionable Connotations

Be aware of language that, to some persons, has questionable racial or ethnic connotations.

While a word or phrase may not be personally offensive to you, it may be to others. As was true in the women's movement, increased awareness convinces people that some words are, indeed, biased. This sensitivity doesn't always come quickly or easily, particularly when words are aimed at someone else.

Following are commonly used words or phrases that have evolved from a Eurocentric, mostly white, culture and have been identified by the Racism and Sexism Resource Center for Educators as having offensive connotations.[4] See the accompanying information for a detailed review of word choices when referring to persons of Spanish cultural heritage.

"Culturally Deprived" or "Culturally Disadvantaged"

These terms may imply superiority of one culture over another. In fact, people so labeled are often bicultural and bilingual. For example:

[4]See Chapter 12 for information on the center's activities.

NO	YES
The company's efforts to assist culturally disadvantaged youths	The company's efforts to assist youths whose family heritage is Spanish, Asian, Black, etc. . . . .

"Nonwhite"

This word implies that white is the standard. In North American language, similar words (such as "nonblack" or "nonyellow") don't exist. For example:

NO	YES
The policy aims to ensure equal treatment of nonwhite personnel.	The policy aims to ensure equal treatment of staff members who are of Asian, Black, etc., heritage.

"Minority"

This word is accurate in North America. However, its use ignores the fact that people of color comprise the majority of the world's population (and may, indeed, comprise the majority in your immediate locale).[5] "Third World" (referring to those nations aligned to neither the United States/Western European sphere nor the Communist Bloc) is receiving increased usage, despite its political overtones. "Minority" will probably remain in common usage, but you may want to consider alternatives. For example:

[5]"Minority" is used throughout this book because our primary audience is North American and because it is commonly used in equal-opportunity laws and affirmative-action policies.

NO	YES
The company's program for minorities	The company's program for employees of Asian, etc., heritage . . . .

"Minority" refers to a group. When the intent is to indicate individuals, use more sensitive, exact wording. Similarly, the communicator should avoid "ethnics."

NO	YES
Women and minorities	Women and members of minority groups; women and minority-group members
Ethnics	Members of ethnic groups; ethnic-group members

"Militant" or "Activist"

Labels such as these two may reveal personal or societal bias. A Black involved in a social protest is called a militant (suggesting violence), while a white counterpart is called an activist (an ideological and political identification).[6]

Be aware of the possible negative implications of color-symbolic words.

Choose language and usage that do not offend people or reinforce bias. In some instances, "black" and "yellow" have become associated with the undesirable or negative. While certain implications are not obviously disparaging, others

[6]Newsday, *Editorial Guidelines* (Garden City: Newsday, 1976), p. 32.

are extremely offensive to some people ("black reputation," "yellow coward").

Patronizing and Tokenism

Avoid patronizing and tokenism toward any racial or ethnic group.

An example of abuse of this guideline is a story on a local charity drive that depicts in words and photographs all poor, sick, and needy citizens as Black, Spanish-surnamed, and so forth. Rarely are Black or Asian volunteers shown ministering to poor or ill whites.

Does your company or organization provide a service such as banking, health care, or education? If so, be alert to stories about special services for largely ethnic communities that say, "We're here to *help* you," rather than, "We're here to *serve* you." As a test, insert the name of a local predominantly white community in your copy. If the story sounds condescending, revise it.

Once-a-year articles or special editions about a particular group may be interpreted as cultural tokenism, especially when such a group constitutes a large part of your company or community. This approach may suggest that a racial or ethnic group is out of the mainstream. Instead, plan for more regular coverage of news, activities, and special events for and about the group.

Substitute substantive information for ethnic clichés.

Too often, communicators try to make a connection that is inappropriate or trite. An example is to stretch for a "pretty" meaning in a

Chinese name. A person of Spanish heritage might prefer to be asked about family history or political experiences, rather than about fiestas. Do more homework. Don't let ethnic clichés substitute for in-depth material.

The Invisible People

Probably the most glaring aspect of bias in media is the almost total absence of Black, Asian, or Spanish-surnamed people. Back-of-the-book material in corporate publications (employee activities and service anniversaries), affirmative-action progress reports, and coverage of ethnic festivals are exceptions.

Yet increasingly, people of all racial and ethnic heritages are holding positions of authority in companies and the community. Many communicators show these new faces in special articles or reports that point out changes and progress. However, a visual balance of all members of the corporate staff or community, on a regular basis, may still be missing.

Review media to see if all groups are fairly represented.

The following checklist might be applied to newspapers, magazines, other publications, advertisements, films, television, and additional media produced by your organization:

- Are persons portrayed in positions of authority almost invariably white?
- Do Asians, Blacks, and so forth, in high-level positions appear only when the communication has an affirmative-action message?
- Are persons of many racial and ethnic groups

proportionately and regularly depicted at all levels in which they hold positions?

- Are Blacks, Asians, and so forth in appropriate positions used as subject-matter experts and/or spokespersons?
- Do your media provide racial and ethnic role models? Is a conscious effort made to do so while pursuing other editorial objectives?

Keep in mind that media should reflect the true makeup of the organization or community. If, for example, no Blacks are in top-management jobs, look for alternatives, and plan coverage that portrays them in the middle management and administrative positions they *do* hold.

SUMMARY

1. Be aware of words, images, and situations that suggest that all or most members of a racial or ethnic group are the same.
2. Avoid qualifiers that reinforce racial and ethnic stereotypes.
3. Identify by race or ethnic origin only when relevant.
4. Be aware of language that, to some persons, has questionable racial or ethnic connotations.
5. Be aware of the possible negative implications of color-symbolic words.
6. Avoid patronizing and tokenism toward any racial or ethnic group.
7. Substitute substantive information for ethnic clichés.
8. Review media to see if all groups are fairly represented.

ADDENDUM ONE:

Selection of Term for Persons of Spanish Cultural Heritage

Many subtleties surround alternate terms to describe persons in North America whose cultural heritage is Spanish. Within the community itself is great diversity and, therefore, differences of opinion exist about the "correct" term.

"Spanish-surnamed" is the most appropriate term currently in use, although many media choose other terms, as do some laws and government publications. It designates people whose names have historical antecedents in the Spanish immigrants who colonized the "New World". Also, it is the broadest term available to identify an extremely diversified (and in many ways, unrelated) group of people. Like other terms, however, it still is not broad enough to distinguish the true heritage of persons who lose or gain a Spanish name by marriage.

To point out how sensitive a judgment this choice is and to provide the communicator with information on which to base such a selection, the following common alternatives and definitions are provided.*

Chicano(a)

Referring only to persons of Mexican descent or heritage who live in the southwestern United

---

*Compiled by Nancy Alvarado, former Manager of Marketing Publications, PCC Business Systems, Santa Ana, CA.

States, it was, until recently, used primarily by the politically active.

Most other Spanish-heritage groups, especially Puerto Ricans, strongly object to the use of Chicano or Chicana to include all Spanish-heritage people. This feeling is most evident outside the Southwest, where other groups of Spanish-heritage people outnumber Chicanos. Older persons of Mexican descent dislike the term because it is a slang word that previously denoted a gangster, and because it is linked to an ideology and militancy they are reluctant to endorse. It is very much a separatist term.

Mexican-American

Again, this term refers to only one segment of a larger ethnic group. It is disliked by many persons who resent being so-called "hyphenated Americans," in spite of being born and reared in the United States. It implies a direct connection with Mexico that doesn't exist for them and it symbolizes exclusion from mainstream America.

Hispano

This word is the choice of people living in New Mexico or people of Spanish heritage other than Mexican. It is sometimes promoted as the best choice for a universal term. However, it is rejected (as being wishy-washy) by those who want to emphasize their Mexican heritage and by those who view the preference for Spanish descent over Mexican-Indian descent as snobbery.

Latino

Preferred by Puerto Ricans and by many Spanish-heritage people from Latin America, it is not commonly used in the southwestern United States but widely used in the East where millions of Spanish-heritage people live. Some persons object to this term because they believe it refers to all Latin-language-based countries, including Italy and France. The word has as much emotional content and is used with as much pride in the East and Midwest as is Chicano in the Southwest.

La Raza

This term has militant overtones. It is not widely used, except in closed gatherings or in political publications. Its use would be resented if employed by an Anglo-Saxon organization or agency to refer to its Spanish-speaking employees or clients. It is racial, not ethnic, in origin but is not extended to Spain, a country considered racially distinct from the genetic mix of Mexico (hence, the snobbishness of some groups).

Emphatically, the term does not describe Native North Americans (North American Indians). Even though the groups seem to overlap, the Native North American and Chicano cultures are distinct and historically antagonistic. By definition, La Raza includes the citizens of the Aztec empire that covered much of the Southwest, Mexico, and Central America.

Spanish-Speaking

Widely used but not strictly accurate, this term may include persons who have learned Spanish as a second language. It excludes the majority of Spanish-heritage people who speak either no Spanish or limited Spanish, and would not classify themselves as fluent in Spanish. The term "monolinguals" is used to identify Latinos who speak English but do not speak any other language.

Spanish-Heritage

Loosely defined, the term includes people who live in the Southwest where Spanish culture has exerted great influence. Too broad and general to carry any emotional impact (which is an advantage), it is also not specific enough to be useful as a definition of any one group. Thus, it is a weak designation that can be offensive.

Spanish-Surnamed

This term includes Filipinos who are not Spanish by culture or race, but only by language. It excludes persons who have changed their names in marriage or whose names are not easily recognizable as being Spanish (for example, Martin, Lugo, or Duran).

ADDENDUM TWO:

Special Considerations in English–French Communication

Communicators in Canada and in the United States whose audience includes residents in the Province of Quebec should be guided by requirements governing the conduct of public relations and internal communication. Canadian communicators who fail to observe them may be fined for noncompliance.

While under no similar legal mandate, United States communicators should use common sense, and communicate in a manner that will not offend or be ineffective.

The following highlights of the law (National Assembly of Quebec Bill 101: Charter of the French Language) pertain to external and internal communication, and became effective in 1977.*

French is the official language of Quebec.

Chapter 1: Introduction, Section 1

This statement is a key one because it indicates that Quebec is *not bilingual*. Rather, French is the recognized language. All other sections of the law are based on this premise.

---

*Compiled by Michael Barrett, Communications Director, Hay Canada, Montreal, PQ.

Catalogues, brochures, folders, and similar publications must be drawn up in French.

Chapter 7: Language of Commerce and Business, Section 53 (External Communications)

News releases are not specifically mentioned but are interpreted to fall under this section of the law.

Contracts, application forms, order forms, invoices, signs, posters, and publications must be drawn up in French.

Sections 55, 57, 58, and 61 (Internal Communications)

The French inscription may be accompanied by a translation in another language; but the translation must not be more prominent than the French.

Section 51

Chapter 2

Regardless of Sex: Toward Communication Free of Sexual Bias

by Loisanne Foerster, ABC[1]

Exciting things have been happening to language in the past half-dozen years, especially language related to sexism. Call it social awareness, call it personal sensitivity, call it natural evolution—but most of all, call it progress. Language usage *is* changing, and this progress favors both men *and* women.

Since sexist language was first called to our attention by early feminists, a growing interest in language theory has developed. Academic studies of how language affects us have increased. The

[1]Patricia Walsh Rao, Director of Advertising for the Pay'n Save Corporation in Seattle, contributed to this chapter in the first edition.

immediate fallout of this work is more attention to language in the media and the willingness of people to discuss and negotiate language-related misunderstandings.

Major newspapers and magazines are reexamining editorial policies that have allowed language discrimination against both sexes. A small but significant and common result is the changing of the "Women's Page" to incorporate all people and their range of interests. Titles such as "People," "You," and "Lifestyles" introduce expanded content in a wide variety of subjects.

Also, modern authors are taking pride in their new verbal sensitivity. For instance, in his very readable, scholarly book *Humankind,* Peter Farb points out that he avoids use of "man" to identify the entire species, except in quotations where it has been used by others:

I have also avoided the grammatical use of masculine pronouns (unless, of course, the male sex is specifically referred to), sex-linked nouns (such as "poetess"), and sex-role stereotypes (such as the assumption that "secretary" is of the female gender). To some readers, my concern may appear exaggerated–but it is valid. This book attempts to get at our essential humanity. It cannot do so if my perspective is distorted and sustained by a male-oriented vocabulary.[2]

Often considered bastions of male supremacy, churches have recently made outstanding contributions to erasing language discrimination. Changes in liturgy, prayers, and theological writings have been announced by Catholics,

[2]Peter Farb, *Humankind* (Boston: Houghton Mifflin, 1978), p. 3.

Protestants, and Jews. "God the Father" has become "God the Creator," and references have been expanded to include women, as well as men.

In business and government, employees and management have worked to change job titles so that they embrace both sexes. "Flight attendants" serve passengers on most airlines. Only stubborn human habit, not company policy, prompts references to "stewardesses." "Firefighters," "letter carriers," and "sales clerks" are among the nondiscriminatory titles we use today without too much mental adjustment. For more information on avoiding sexism on the job, see Chapter 5.

Early antagonists warned that attempts to be nonsexist would result in clumsy or ineffectual language. Farb and others have proven them wrong. Some new words suggested to replace existing pronouns *were* awkward. "S/he" and "herm" were never accepted, while using "they" as a singular pronoun has become a popular interim solution (much to the dismay of grammarians). Also, creative communicators are rewriting sentences with less difficulty than monotonously repeating the cumbersome phrase, "he or she."

Some stumbling has, of course, occurred along the way, because language is generated more by ritual than by thought. Even the most careful communicators listen with horror to their own voices repeating hackneyed, insensitive phrases. We can sympathize with the obviously aware conference speaker who told his mixed audience, "I want all of you *men* and *people* to understand what I'm saying."

In his case, as in our own, the attempt is significant. At least we are trying to change old language habits (even if unsuccessfully) and trying to understand and take responsibility for both the overt and the covert messages we communicate.

We strive for accuracy and quality in our work and do not deliberately slight, slur, or misrepresent any person or group through the language we use. However, changing business practices and social patterns (which include women in increasing numbers in areas previously off-limits to them) make certain language habits obsolete. Heightened personal awareness and sensitivity to possible language bias are necessary for today's communicators.

Guidelines in this chapter can be the base for recognizing (and thus avoiding) sexual bias in language.[3] They are presented as suggestions and translated into human terms by communicators who share personal experiences and observations.

Personhood

I am a shareholder in a major corporation, a leader in an industry that is vitally important to society. I do not question the achievements of this company, neither its financial growth nor its product integrity. I do, however, question the attitudes it may have toward some of its employees, as reflected in its annual report.

I was drawn to a particular photo of a woman operating the controls of some sophisticated equipment. The cutline read, "In the control room of the highly automated plant, women staff members *(emphasis mine) monitor every aspect of operations."*

---

[3]Much of this material is based on McGraw-Hill Book Company, *Guidelines for Equal Treatment of the Sexes in McGraw-Hill Book Company Publications* (New York: McGraw-Hill, 1974).

The photo and cutline stuck out like a sore thumb. The ones featuring men clearly identified each individual, no matter how menial his job.

The difference may have been an oversight, but it told me something about the company. If men in the annual report are recognized as individuals but women are not, what does this distinction indicate about the motives, the feelings of the decision-makers toward female employees?

Are women treated as full, contributing members of the staff–or as something else? If I were a woman, I'd feel rather uncomfortable working there.

Bob Buskirk, Public Relations Manager
United Telephone Company of Iowa
Newton, Iowa

The most subtle form of sexism is the omission of women in references that take in humanity at large. Using the word "man" to describe men in particular, as well as humanity as a whole, began with translation of the Latin word for our genus ("Homo") into English. Adoption of the so-called generic pronoun "he" followed automatically. This practice is potentially offensive to at least half of any communicator's audience.

Include all people in general references by substituting asexual words and phrases for man-words.

Here are some examples of substitute wording:

NO	YES
Mankind	People, humanity, human beings, human race, humankind

Man-made	Synthetic, artificial, constructed, manufactured, of human origin
Manpower	Human resources, human energy, workers, workforce
Man-sized	Husky, sizable, large, requiring exceptional ability
Man-hours	Hours, total hours, staff-hours, working hours *or, specifically,* Secretarial hours, shop-hours, engineering hours, driver-hours
Founding fathers (other than when referring to members of the U.S. First Continental Congress)	Pioneers, colonists, patriots, forebears, founders
Gentlemen's agreement	Informal agreement, your word, a handshake, oral contract
Layman, layman's terms	Lay, common, ordinary, informal

Communicate to both male and female reference points.

Here are some examples of alternatives to a male-only perspective:

NO	YES
Employees and their wives (With living-together arrangements now, this phrase takes on additional risk of inaccuracy.)	Employees and their spouses, employees and their guests

The man on the way up	The person, employee, or executive on the way up
The lady of the house	The homemaker, the consumer
The man on the street, the common man	Everyone, the average person

Use collective pronouns that recognize both sexes.

Common methods for avoiding the masculine pronoun in collective references are the phrase "he or she" or the plural pronoun "they" in a singular sense. The former is often clumsy; the latter, grammatically incorrect. Stubborn insistence that the pronouns "he," "him," and "his" stand for all people can create misunderstandings, as well as ill feelings. Consider this sentence from a group insurance brochure: "If an employee becomes pregnant while covered under this policy, *he* will be entitled to . . ."

To avoid using male-only pronouns,

- Reword the sentence to eliminate unnecessary gender pronouns.
- Recase the sentence into the plural.
- Replace masculine pronouns with "one" or "you," as appropriate.
- Alternate use of female and male pronouns.

NO	YES
Each employee completes his timesheet at the end of his shift and hands it to his supervisor.	Each employee completes a timesheet at the end of the shift and hands it to the supervisor.
	or
	All employees complete their timesheets at the end

of their shifts and hand them to their supervisors.

or

Complete your timesheet at the end of your shift and hand it to your supervisor.

or

Each employee completes a timesheet at the end of his or her shift and hands it to her or his supervisor.

Titles

Concern about sexism in titles arises in two areas: courtesy titles and job titles. The following information elaborates on the influence that equal and respectful use of these titles can have on the communication and reception of messages.

Courtesy Titles

My name is Pat: P-A-T, a common name for a woman or a man. But people who don't know which I am consistently tack "Mr." in front of it.

I could eliminate some of the confusion by using Patricia, Patty, or Trish; but these variations are not my name. Men and women with names such as Lynn, Connie, or Chris probably have the same problem, as do people who use their initials.

Does a business letter, newspaper article, or speech introduction require reference to sex or marital status? Why not use just first and last names or last names only?

What I object to is the apparent assumption that, because I'm in business, I must be a man—and the subtle implication that my sex or marital status determines my worth.

Pat Risley, Director of Publications
University of Houston
Houston, Texas

The meanings of "master" and "mistress" (from which "Mr." and "Mrs." evolved) have changed over the years. At one time, these courtesy titles were reserved for persons of a specific high rank or honor. Where "master" once preceded a man's name as a sign of honor, it is now used only for boys under 12 and retained as part of certain titles (such as "court master" in Canada) as a mark of respect. The honorific "mistress" has fallen into disrepute.

Other titles (such as "squire," "goodman," "goodwife," and "maid") have been used and discarded in English-speaking history, leaving only today's titles. The abbreviated derivatives of "Mr.," "Mrs.," and "Miss" were gradually bestowed upon all men and women because, in the days of strict decorum, using last names with titles was the rule. To some degree, calling people of brief acquaintance by their first names is not socially acceptable, even now.

But these courtesy titles didn't evolve equally for women and men. "Mr." designates all adult males and implies no rank or status. However, "Mrs." and "Miss" distinguish women according to marital status. "Ms." now seeks to show that this distinction is not important in most cases.

As society becomes more relaxed, use of titles gets even more confusing. In some instances,

"Mr." is dropped before a man's name, but "Mrs." or "Miss" is retained before a woman's ("Parker received the award from Mrs. Adler."). Other accepted styles grant a man his full name, while referring to a woman by her first name only or by title and last name ("Steven Parker received the award from Janet" or ". . . from Mrs. Adler."). Eliminate such unequal and potentially offensive treatment by following this single guideline:

Refer to women and men equally and make references consistent.

Use full names in first references and first or last names only in later references. When courtesy titles are used, apply them equally to men and women. For example:

NO	YES
Sam Purdy and Miss Brown	Sam Purdy and Julia Brown
Julia and Purdy	Julia and Sam, Brown and Purdy
Mr. Purdy and Julia	Sam and Julia, Purdy and Brown
Miss Brown and Sam	Miss (or Ms.) Brown and Mr. Purdy

A married, divorced, or widowed woman may use her husband's name, her family name, or both. Ask her which she prefers ("Jane Smith," "Jane Smith Jones," "Jane Smith-Jones" or "Jane Jones").

Style established by your organization may require that courtesy titles be used in first and subsequent references. Ask women what titles they prefer or, as an alternative, *consistently* refer to them as "Ms." For example:

NO	YES
Sam Purdy and Julia Brown were recently promoted. Purdy has been with the firm since 1965, and Julia joined us in 1973.	Sam Purdy and Julia Brown were recently promoted. Purdy has been with the firm since 1965, and Brown joined us in 1973.
	or
	Mr. Purdy has been with the firm since 1965, and Ms. Brown joined us in 1973.
	or
	Sam has been with the firm since 1965, and Julia joined us in 1973.

Job Titles

"I wish I could ride around the park on a horsie," my daughter Sheela said wistfully, reminiscing about her day at the park and the tall police officer she saw astride an even taller horse.

"Well, Sheela," I replied, "perhaps when you grow up you can do just that. You can join the mounted police and help patrol our parks."

"No, I can't," she said firmly. The trace of anger in her young face surprised me.

"Why not?"

"Because I'm not a boy. And you have to be a boy to be a policeman."

*"But Sheela, there are police*women, *too."*

*"No there aren't. I never saw one. And I've never heard of one, I just hear police*man. *Police*man. *Police*man."

No amount of argument changed her mind. For the next several days, at every opportunity, she pointed out evidence to support her conclusion. I found almost nothing to refute her. At the age of four, she had already limited her horizons because of sexist language and because of a lack of role models.

Patricia Walsh Rao, Director of Advertising
Pay'n Save Corporation
Seattle, Washington

Continual use of nongeneric titles reinforces assumptions that women and men are restricted to certain roles. It inaccurately identifies and presents a false image of people and their jobs.

Substitute neutral words for "man" or "woman" in job titles.

Most titles carry the male designation through usage. "Fireman," "mailman," and "foreman" have been written into contracts and job descriptions for years. However, changes are being made, and titles such as "firefighter," "postal carrier," and "supervisor" are just as easily understood. For example:

NO	YES
Businessman, businesswoman	Business executive, manager, entrepreneur
Chairman, chairwoman	Presiding officer, the chair, head, leader, coordinator, moderator
Workman	Laborer, employee, staff member, worker
Foreman	Supervisor, manager
Repairman, handyman	Maintenance worker
	or, specifically,

	Plumber, electrician, carpenter
Cameraman	Camera operator, technician, photographer
Delivery boy	Porter, carrier, courier, messenger
Salesman, sales girl	Sales clerk, sales representative

The practice of changing a title ending in "man" to one ending in "person" can result in a word that sounds forced and clumsy. Also, the new composite word is often used for women only, implying even more strongly that reference is made to a woman in a man's position. If you use the suffix "person," do so consistently. For example:

NO	YES
The sales manager supervises six salesmen and one salesperson.	The sales manager supervises seven salespersons. *or* The sales manager supervises a sales staff of seven.

"Man" suffixes are accurate when the person is a man, just as "woman" is accurate when the opposite is true. However, use a neutral word when sexual makeup is mixed or unknown.

Stereotypes

Our first television production was done in the studio of a local equipment dealer. Inexperience with this medium gave the photographer, another writer, and me a feeling of adventure. For two days, we got acquainted with the equipment, and on the third, we produced a half-hour tape. We began in ignorance and emerged with a program that eventually helped sell management on installing our own visual-communication center. Only creative accomplishment, from idea to fulfillment, brings the kind of joy we three shared.

The sales manager of the studio sensed our excitement and joined in our self-congratulations. One by one, he spoke to us.

"Bob," he said, shaking the hand of the man who had worked the control console, "you make a great director." I nodded in silent agreement.

"Jerry," he exclaimed, patting the back of the man who had run the other camera, "you got some terrific shots."

My turn was next. My smile got wider as he approached, and I felt the spot on my back where his congratulatory pat would land.

"And darling," he cooed, hugging me in a most familiar embrace, "you added a spot of beauty to our studio." My joy flowed out through the wound in my heart. My hard work, my creative energy, my contributions to the finished program—none of them mattered. I was, after all, a woman and only responsive to remarks about my looks.

Loisanne Foerster, ABC
Director, Foerst Place
Crozet, Virginia

"Gee whiz! Isn't it amazing what some girls can do?"

Of course, few communicators are that blatant in references to women's contributions to their companies or communities. But many convey a gee-whiz attitude in their choice of words.

Women, as well as men, are guilty of such stereotyping—against both sexes. Communication based on stereotypic assumptions is inaccurate, distorting, and offensive.

Use parallel language when referring to persons by sex.

Females over the age of 18 are women, not girls or gals (unless men are referred to as boys or guys). Women should be called ladies only when men are called gentlemen. Skewed references support stereotypic attitudes. For example:

NO	YES
The ladies and the men	The women and the men; the ladies and the gentlemen; the girls and the boys; the guys and the gals
Man and wife	Husband and wife

Grant equal respect to both women and men.

Do not trivialize either sex. Don't describe men by mental attributes or professional position while describing women by physical attributes or social position. Do not depict men as bumbling in personal relationships or as sissies when they are sensitive to feelings. For example:

NO	YES
John Simon is a competent executive, and his wife Ann is a charming brunette.	The Simons make an attractive couple. John is a handsome blond, and Ann is a striking brunette.

or	or
Ann Simon is a successful designer, but her husband John wears the pants in the family.	Ann and John Simon are highly respected in their fields. She is a successful designer, and he is a competent attorney.
He cried like a woman.	He cried.

Treat women with respect by eliminating the use of a patronizing or girl-watching tone. Do not resort to sexual innuendoes, jokes, or puns about either men or women; if the story can't stand without them, it shouldn't be pursued. Avoid portraying women as typically weak, helpless, or hysterical, or men as typically strong, brave, or rational. Do not degrade women's concerns or issues; they're as legitimate as those of men.

Avoid using expressions such as "women's libber" when referring to women who have gotten ahead. The term "women's lib" was coined as a shortened version of "the women's liberation movement." Frequently used in a disparaging way, it often calls up visions of hysterical, militant women who care nothing about the opinions of others. Most feminists and egalitarians of both sexes fail to fit this picture. Look for the qualities that set people apart as individuals and find a more interesting and factual story. For example:

NO	YES
The girls (for females over 18)	The women
The little lady, the better half	Wife, partner
Girl Friday	Secretary, assistant

Libber, women's lib	Feminist, liberationist, women's movement
Coed (for female student at a coeducational school)	Student, woman
Ladylike	Well-mannered
Housewife	Homemaker; consumer, customer, or shopper (in an economic sense)
Career girl	Refer to the woman's profession or title ("Professor Joan Temple"; "Lucia Johansen, construction worker")
Cleaning woman	Housekeeper, custodian
Authoress, poetess	Author, poet

One of the most subtle stereotypes of women occurs in audio communication. When radio spots, slide narrations, and other audio media consistently use men as "the voice of authority" and women as "the lighter touch" (when they're used at all), stereotypes are perpetuated. In addition to habit, such usage is based on the assumption that a male voice is more pleasing because of its lower pitch.

As a communicator, your objective is to get across a message. Male *and* female voices can sell, convince, or entertain, while being pleasing to the ear. Listen to several audition tapes and select an announcer or narrator on the basis of ability to handle the material. If your audio need is extensive, use voice differences to your advantage by alternating female and male voices to help hold listener attention.

Belittling

Marlo Thomas, why didn't you and your friends write "Free To Be You and Me" when I was growing up? Now, like a lot of people, I'm playing catch-up with the whole movement of humanism, equality, and self-actualization.

I'd like to change a lot of things in this world, but particularly put-downs, the little demeaning statements that unaware people make casually. These constant comments bore into my soul like water torture. Consider . . .

. . . The executive visiting my company's hospitality suite at a trade-association meeting who asks, "And whose letters do you type?"

. . . The clerk in the camera shop who doesn't believe that the film to be developed is mine: "Well, what's your boss's name?"

. . . The man who announces loudly when in mixed company, "I'd rather sit next to this pretty girl."

. . . And the woman who says, "I'm not a women's libber, but . . ." and goes on to lament an injustice we all want to correct.

I keep trying to fashion a defense against these put-downs. Maybe, someday, I won't have to bother.

Cynthia Simone, Editor
Chevron U.S.A.
San Francisco, California

Base communication on pertinent qualities, not on sex.

Under affirmative-action goals, more and more women and minority-group members are being promoted and recognized for their contributions. As a consequence, many organizations want to emphasize that they are following positive hiring and promoting practices.

But stories about the first woman in a traditionally male occupation (or vice versa) may emphasize, instead, the company's previous lack of recognition. They also construct additional stumbling blocks for featured employees by making them stand out: One-of-a-kind employees are often expected to do better than the norm.

Common sense should rule all writing and editing. Not communicating about women—or men—as a way of avoiding sexism is discrimination, too. Here are some alternatives:

NO	YES
A television program featuring the only girl on a championship high-school basketball team.	Base the feature on the team's struggle for success and how everyone, including the girl, contributed.
An article on the first female dentist to serve on the national board of her association.	Find some other angle, such as her unique campaign for the post or her small-town practice, as opposed to the metropolitan practices of other board members.

Labels

I had just been through one of the most frustrating interviews of my life. The man I had been directed to as an expert on my subject was reluctant to give me any positive information and finally refused to make a decisive comment. He was a person who could not make a comprehensive statement regarding his own thought processes or opinions.

An hour later, I was in a meeting, fighting for a program I had originated. I laid out my plan point by logical point, countering each negative statement with positive proof that this project would be good for the company. I supported my statements with facts, figures, and precedents, and won my case.

Later, a former opponent complimented me. "Honey," he said, "you think like a man."

I recalled my earlier experience and was struck by the paradox. Stereotypic labels live on, despite so many visible exceptions to prove them invalid.

Mary Ann Coffey, Attorney at Law
New Orleans, Louisiana

All men are not strong, heroic, or logical. All women are not empty-headed, afraid of snakes, or noncompetitive. Everyone *knows* these things, but we often communicate as if we don't.

Labels, like clichés, make communicating simple—we don't have to think and neither does our reader or viewer. Employing phrases such as "just like a man" or "just like a woman" allows people to apply their own favorite prejudices.

Avoid labels that limit either sex.

Each person is different, and careful communicators reflect this fact in their work.

Assumptions about where men and women "belong" lead to unequal practices in reporting about both. Many communicators feel compelled to announce the sex of a woman in business, but not that of a man ("executive and lady executive" or "manager and woman manager"). Similarly, men become the oddities when we use labels such as "male secretary" or "male nurse."

This distinction perpetuates the myth that certain jobs or responsibilities are reserved for men and others for women. It singles out the person who deviates from the norm and discourages a feeling of equal opportunity.

Similarly limiting is the practice of labeling projects as "women's work" or as "a job for a man." Note the limitations created by these qualifiers: "She handled the forklift *as well as a man*," or "He takes care of his children *as well as any man could*."

Look beyond words or ideas that label and limit. Consider the tone of the entire communication. For example:

NO	YES
A story on a woman who, as a manager, somehow keeps up with the shopping and cooking, along with her duties as department head.	Stick to business. Imagine depicting a man who is able to keep up with the shopping and cooking while still getting ahead on his job.
An article that shows male employees as having only "manly" outside interests (such as hunting or drag racing).	Look for a balance of interests in all subjects. Show as natural a man who studies yoga or knits.
Special sections "for women only" that offer recipes, sewing tips, and fashion news.	Women are not really that narrow in their interests. Offer a variety of material to women *and* men.

SUMMARY

1. Include all people in general references by substituting asexual words and phrases for man-words.
2. Communicate to both male and female reference points.
3. Use collective pronouns that recognize both sexes.
4. Refer to women and men equally and make references consistent.
5. Substitute neutral words for "man" or "woman" in job titles.
6. Use parallel language when referring to persons by sex.
7. Grant equal respect to both women and men.
8. Base communication on pertinent qualities, not on sex.
9. Avoid labels that limit either sex.

Chapter 3

Regardless of Age: Toward Communication Sensitive to Older People and Children

by Lucille DeView

At some time in our lives, each of us is "young" and "old." But when we age beyond our youth, we tend to forget language that abused us as children. And until we are advanced in years, we seem oblivious to ways language metes out a similar fate to older people.

In the brief history of equal-opportunity regulations, mandates against age discrimination came later than those against racism and sexism. Only recently, then, has the role of language in support of equal treatment for both older people *and* children emerged as a concern in North America.

This chapter explores how our language affects both extremes of the age spectrum. First, it examines the more common occurrence of abuse: discrimination against older people. Second, it offers guidelines for bias-free communication about children.

Unlike other forms of discrimination that may touch certain individuals lightly, ageism has no spectators. At any given time, you, a member of your family, or a friend can be the target of blatant or subtle bias in newspapers, magazines, radio, television, films, and everyday conversation. Thus, each of us has a vested interest in developing a sensitivity to language and age, which is the objective of this information.

Older People

"Old and crotchety?" No, sir and madam, not so; a canard pure and simple . . . . I like "old and full of wisdom." Or maybe "boldly old," you think?[1]

Katharine Barry
Retired office worker

Don't use the word "elderly" to me. I'm in that bracket. I know that. But I don't accept it . . . . I think young.[2]

Hildegarde
Singer and actress

The prejudice against the old is overwhelming, but not without its irony. People who are prejudiced never become the source of their

---

[1]Katharine Barry, "My Turn," *Newsweek*, August 11, 1980, p. 13.
[2]*The Boston Globe*, March 4, 1980, p. 25.

attacks: A chauvinist never becomes a woman; a racist never becomes a Black; an anti-Semite never becomes a Jew. And yet we continue with an attitude that the old are inferior. On reaching old age, we may be prejudiced against ourselves![3]

Dr. *Alex Comfort*
Geriatrics specialist and author
The Joy of Sex

We want to see a more positive image of ourselves. In all media, we like to be shown as intelligent human beings.[4]

Sadie S. Platcow
Writer for The Elder

Society and the North American media don't treat older people well: too much patronizing, too much stereotyping, too many stories dwelling on the problems and foibles of old age, and too few about its joys and rewards.

A strange disparity exists between the realities of the later years and our images of what we think those years will be like. In the news, we see active older persons as revered rulers, Nobel Prize winners, leading actors, explorers, educators, and thinkers, at the height of wisdom and ability. Yet when *communicators* portray old age, they invariably describe it as a time of waning physical and mental powers typified by canes and wheelchairs and persons who are child-like, self-indulgent, helpless, and a bother to have around.

Writers label and limit with words. They refer

---

[3]*The Times-Picayune*, October 12, 1980, pp. III-8.
[4]Sadie S. Platcow, private interview, November 10, 1980.

to later years as "twilight" or "sunset" years, though twilight and sunset come to young and old alike. For many, "dawns" and "sunrises" fill aging with excitement and new adventures.

Small wonder, then, that activists are rebelling against these stereotypes by declaring "Senior Power!" and "Old Is Better!" They speak for an age group that is growing larger every year. Today, one out of every nine people in the United States (24 million-plus) is age 65 or older. By the turn of the century, that number is expected to increase to one out of every six. And by the year 2030, more persons will be over 65 than under 25.[5]

Communicators must respond to this varied and vital segment of the population by portraying its members with accuracy and sensitivity—and without bias.

Labels

Designate age only when relevant.

In most stories, age is irrelevant. Yet news style insists that it be given: "Mary Jones, 58, attended a business conference." "Bill and Edna Brown, both 82, celebrated the holidays with daughter Louise Brown, 59." Drop age in cases such as these.

When five residents of a small group home are each more than 100 years old, however, age is relevant and should be given with their names.

Use terms other than "senior citizen"; ask groups or individuals what they prefer to be called.

Among groups in the United States that consider "senior citizen" euphemistic are the

---

[5]U.S. Bureau of the Census statistics.

National Gray Panthers, American Association of Retired Persons, and National Retired Teachers Association. They prefer "older person," "older people," or "older American."

Feelings can be intense. One Florida editor recalls that a "Senior Citizens Day" failed miserably because, organizers confessed, they shouldn't have used that term.

"Elderly" is not as objectionable, though it is not really accurate when it includes persons in their 50s, as it often does.

"Oldster" has the same diminutive quality as "youngster"—except that children *are* diminutive, and older persons are not.

"Mature individual" is sometimes used, but it describes an emotional or psychological quality (maturity) more than an age group. A younger person might be mature, while an older one might not be.

"Golden ager" is sometimes useful, though some people think it even more euphemistic than "senior citizen."

When in doubt, ask groups and individuals what they prefer to be called. Many older people abhor some of the terms just mentioned; others don't mind. "Senior citizen" appears in the names of clubs and housing developments, but their members or residents may prefer not to use it to describe themselves directly in the text of a story. Always ask.

Use words that accurately describe older people.

"Grandmotherly" and "grandfatherly" have an old-fashioned ring, suggesting Grandma doling out cookies and Grandpa rocking on the veranda (though many never do either). Today, being "grandmotherly" or "grandfatherly" could mean something entirely different.

A recent survey of grandfathers in the United States showed that most keep fit jogging, walking, or doing yoga. One in four surveyed was an active swimmer; one in five regularly cycled; one in four was an ardent dancer (most preferring ballroom steps but some opting for disco).[6]

Since "grandmotherly" and "grandfatherly" aren't accurate descriptions, avoid their use. Do not, however, ignore the grandparent role when relevant to the story. This status is generally a source of pride and should be included with all the other "roles" that comprise the whole person. But in some cases—in career stories, for example—mentioning family relationships is not relevant and, therefore, not appropriate.

Use the name of the person to avoid stereotyping into the grandparent role. For example:

NO	YES
The 60-ish Chicago grandmother gushed when meeting her idol.	Mary Green was thrilled to meet her singer-idol, whom she first saw perform in the 30s when she was in her teens. (Note: She didn't "gush.")

Avoid terms such as "spry." Lydia Bragger, Chairwoman of the National Gray Panthers Media Watch, points out that to say one person is "spry" implies others in that age group are not. The Watch receives an average of 10 complaints each

[6]*Family Circle*, December 16, 1980, p. 36.

week reporting such abuses as a news story about inflation that referred to the "drones" on Social Security getting their raises.[7]

Labels that especially stereotype older women can be corrected as follows:[8]

NO	YES
Passive, dependent, frivolous, shrewish, nagging	She enjoys buying presents and beautiful clothes.
	She insists that everyone in the family share in chores, which must be done on time.

Myths

Don't be amazed at the endurance of older people.

A story about a woman who farms several hundred acres and raises chickens, hogs, and cattle, ends: "Not bad for a 60-year-old widow!" This example is typical of a gee-whiz attitude toward anyone past 50 who drives a car, skis, or continues a career. None of these activities is unusual.

Life expectancy will climb from 73 years today in the United States to an expected 85 years in the near future (with one group, white women, almost at that figure now). As more and more people stay healthy and active longer, communicators have

---

[7]Lydia Bragger, private interview, November 8, 1980.

[8]Mary E. Spencer, *Truth About Aging: Guidelines for Publishers* (Washington: National Retired Teachers Association and American Association of Retired Persons, 1979).

less and less excuse for presenting physical activities and accomplishments as extraordinary.

Recognize that older persons are individuals.

No such thing as "acting your age" exists. Grandmother Honey sews, bakes, and seldom leaves her home. Uncle Jack and Aunt Milly go to the horse races every Wednesday. Cousin John is a lay minister.

Older people find as many ways to spend a day as younger people. The variety is infinite and should be communicated.

Draw upon the fact that many of their lives have spanned the era from horse and buggy to lunar landing craft. But also recognize that others prefer to talk about their interests in computer technology or county government.

Reflect the variety of appearance of older persons.

The bent, twisted body with thick glasses, a toothless smile, bald or sparse gray hair, and too much or too little weight is not an accurate picture of all older people. In fact, the real picture is more often of a trim body maintained by exercise and sound eating habits, carefully styled hair, fashionable glasses, and a toothy grin.

Show fewer people in baggy, dark, worn, out-of-date clothes. Show more who dress attractively in colorful, well-fitting garments. Though older people don't usually try to emulate younger people in appearance, reflect in what your viewers see the pants suits, down vests, t-shirts, and jeans that are the easy-care choice of many.

For more guidance in depicting older persons, see Chapter 6.

Stress that age doesn't necessarily bring loneliness and an end to sexual interest.

Write more of togetherness than of loneliness, more of affection than disinterest.

Among older Americans, 74 percent of men and 35 percent of women live with spouses. Another 23 percent of women live with relatives or unrelated persons, as do 7 percent of men. The number living alone is increasing — 36 percent of women, 14 percent of men. This arrangement is often by choice more than circumstance, as a way to be independent.[9]

Many older people who do live alone require special services. Women especially need such things as to-the-door transportation. More communities are becoming aware of these special needs and organizing to meet them. Communicators can help tell this side of the story —but present it as only one side.

Show realistic living arrangements. They are varied: married couples; older people living with their children, with unrelated persons or in group homes; single people in their own homes or apartments; unmarried couples; relatives living together; the "extended family" of friends of all ages.

The myth about older people and loneliness or sexual interest is contradicted in the media by such examples as the reporting in 1980 of the sinking of a cruise ship in the chilly waters off Alaska. Most of those aboard were older people on a retirement cruise.

Men and women were separated during the evacuation so that days elapsed before couples were reunited. The media did a commendable job,

---

[9]Ibid, p. 10.

in writing and photography, of sensitively reporting the tremendous outpouring of genuine affection that was expressed at the end of the ordeal.

Reality

Present age fairly and realistically.

In the zeal to encourage a positive attitude toward retirement, media sometimes exaggerate the amount of money and leisure activities one can expect. The absence of any reference to stress or occasional difficulties in such stories makes them misleading fantasies.

Be fair and realistic. No age is all fun. Many older people enjoy fishing, for example, but more fish off the pier than from charter boats. Also, going bowling or dancing doesn't preclude shoveling snow, repairing the washer, and paying bills.

Older people may visit sick friends and attend funerals, but they also have more time for socializing and closeness, something many younger people envy. Examples of realism are

- A TV commercial for a bus company showing an older couple enjoying their low-budget trip.
- An older woman at a microphone leading a rally in a neighborhood zoning dispute.

Balance "problem" stories with more positive experiences. When most messages are about loneliness, poverty, illness, and distress, old age becomes something to dread. Don't avoid or gloss over such subjects. As a communicator, you have a responsibility to alert society and help find solutions. Your audience, however, needs to know that life in the later years can also be very good. Examples of positive stories:

- 50th wedding anniversaries that include a description of how the anniversary was celebrated, as well as what life was like at the time of the wedding.
- Back-to-school stories showing older persons who continue to learn and get degrees.

Tell the true health story of older people.

Statistics prove that people live longer, healthier lives than the preponderance of nursing-home and hospital stories would have us believe. We see so many older persons in TV commercials hobbling painfully up stairways or rubbing muscles and swollen joints that we accept such maladies as the norm—but they are not.

Avoid making ill health worse than it is. While serious medical conditions limit major activities for some 45 percent of our older population, these people are far from "invalids." Most learn to cope well and manage to be independent, enjoying life, despite their physical limitations.

Although many older people need health care for longer periods of time than do younger people, they do recover, and most hospital stays are temporary. Realize, as gerontologists tell us, that older people become ill because they are sick, not because they are old.

Fewer than 5 percent of all older people in the United States reside in nursing homes. However, the number of stories about them leads us to believe the percentage is much higher.[10] Do not

---

[10]Ibid.

ignore these people when attention is warranted, but consider doing some educating at the same time. For example:

NO	YES
He is confined to a nursing home.	He is a nursing-home resident, one of the less than 5 percent of older people who require such care.

Communicate about such services as visiting nurses, home companions, and programs for caring for the terminally ill at home. Find inspiring examples of persons who have overcome limitations. For instance:

- An older man with multiple sclerosis who was voted "citizen of the year" for his leadership in neighborhood rehabilitation.
- An older woman who had lost her sight but continued to be an effective and much-loved Brownie and Girl Scout leader.

Be especially sensitive to the needs of older women.

Communicators can take guidance from such groups as The Older Women's League, which educates the public in the United States about special needs of this fastest-growing and poorest segment of our population.[11] Some facts:

- Their average income in 1979 was $59 per week ($106 for older men).

---

[11]Statistics of The Older Women's League Educational Fund, New Voice for Middle Years and Older Women. See Chapter 12 for more information.

- Their poverty rate is 65 percent higher than that of older men.
- One-third of all widows live below the poverty line; only 2 percent collect their husband's pensions. (The average age of widowhood is 56; one of every two women can expect to be a widow at 65 or later.)
- A full half of all women now working are in jobs with no pensions. Older women work at the lowest-paid jobs with lowest benefits.
- The ratio of women to men over age 65 is 10 to 6.

These facts should be reported frequently so that needs are identified and met.

Patronizing

Use words that do not patronize or demean older people.

Many of the words we use out of habit are insulting to older people and further encourage a lack of respect.[12] For example:

NO	YES
Cute, sweet, dear, little	She has endeared herself to the neighborhood with her years of kindly concern and daily deeds.
Crippled, deaf, dentured, emaciated, feeble, fragile, frail, frowning, gray, inactive, wrinkled, withered, dirty, doddering	He has been in poor health for some years, and his hearing is impaired.

[12]Spencer, *Truth About Aging*, pp. 18–19.

Cheerless, dull, eccentric, foolish, morose, meek, obstinate, queer, sad, senile	He was never a particularly cheery person. She is an original thinker. At times, he feels discouraged. She has great determination.
Old maid, old codger, old biddy, fuddy duddy, lecher, old fool, Geritol generation, has-been, over the hill, out of date, fading fast	She has enjoyed her single lifestyle. He has always been meticulous about his appearance. She likes rock music, as well as the oldies.

Recognize that older people are not "old babies."

"Open a newspaper or magazine and you're hit with 'Senior citizens must be taught to cook properly and should also learn which foods are the most wholesome,' " says retired office worker Katharine Barry. "We are the experienced shoppers and the experienced housekeepers . . . . These college gals with their newly won degrees and swollen egos—how they patronize us hapless 'babies.' "[13]

The National Center for Health Statistics in the United States confirms her claims about nutrition. Only 42 percent of the 20-to-34 age group breakfast daily, while 86 percent of the over-65 group never miss this most important meal of the day. As for the unnutritious habit of snacking, 43

[13]Barry, *Newsweek*.

percent of those 20 to 34 snack daily; 80 percent of those over 65 never do.

Effusiveness and baby talk are very patronizing. Ms. Barry reports a young woman said to her at a church supper, "Just stay put, dear. We don't want you getting lost, do we? And don't get too hungry; din-din won't be ready for a few minutes."

Another aspect of the cruise-ship sinking mentioned earlier is that all aboard survived, despite the adversity of weather and a night in lifeboats. Many news reports termed their safe return to shore "miraculous."

Others, however, accurately pointed out that the older people responded to the emergency, en masse, with a strong sense of survival developed over many years of riding out the ups and downs of living. The media rightly asked, "Would younger people have done as well?"

The Invisible Age

Include older persons in mainstream stories.

More men and women over 55 watch TV than any other age group. But only one out of every 50 fictional television characters is over 65. Older women (except in "soaps" and "specials") are rarely shown in romantic roles. Older men are more often seen as villains or unlikeable characters.[14]

Commercials and print ads portray older people as chronically ill, martyred, and hard of hearing. They are also often desperately in need of advice or all too willing to give it to younger people.

---

[14]*Newsweek,* November 12, 1979, p. 124.

In all media, older people appear primarily in stories about their own age group. A newspaper, for example, may include older persons in a feature about nursing homes or a dance at a community center, but exclude them from interviews about politics, solar energy, world hunger, or the local art show.

Realize that older readers and viewers don't want to be segregated, but rather included in the mainstream of life. Present realistic portrayals of this age group in plays, commercials, stories, and articles. Include older people with the general population in opinion surveys and interviews. Acknowledge the thoughts, feelings, intelligence, and individuality of older persons in stories that show respect.

Include employed older persons in stories.

When entertainer Hildegarde was asked why, in her 70s, she had not retired, she replied, "Do you think that I look as if I belong in a rocking chair? Do you think that I should be playing croquet at Palm Beach?"[15] The elegant photo accompanying the story clearly said "no." She definitely belonged on stage.

Approximately 15 percent of all over-65 Americans are employed full-time, a figure expected to rise with liberalized retirement laws. More older people are also now taking part-time jobs to supplement incomes and utilize their talents.[16]

Few communicators, however, feature older persons in a work setting in manufacturing plants or as clerks, doctors, lawyers, small-business

---

[15]*Boston Globe*.

[16]U.S. Department of Labor statistics.

owners, artists, nurses, and the like. In addition to telling their stories, such media attention may help increase the number of jobs for older people. Some 46 percent of retirees in the United States say they would like to be working. And 48 percent of employees ages 50 to 64 say they intend to keep working beyond age 65.[17]

Do more stories about agencies that specialize in placing older workers. Detail the advantages of hiring them, including lower absenteeism, more efficient performance, and fewer accident or disability problems than other age groups.

Also, report the special job needs of older women, the largest group in the lowest-income category.

Stress action and involvement of older people.

The media do an excellent job of encouraging healthful recreation and providing information on social events. As a result, more people are getting involved, and communicators have no excuse for portraying older people as bored, sedentary, down-hearted, or passively watching the world go by.

Focus on the majority who play tennis, ski, dance, jog, golf, cycle, and go to concerts. Deemphasize the smaller number who must confine themselves to playing cards, watching TV, knitting, and sewing.

Older people vote more conscientiously than any other age group, and some 25 percent do volunteer community work and promote cherished causes.[18] Include their enthusiasm and

---

[17] Ibid.

[18] Spencer, *Truth About Aging*, p. 13.

caring in your media and talk less about the few who don't participate.

Through religion and service, many older people nourish the inner person, along with the physical and emotional aspects of their lives. Incorporate this element in articles and other communication.

The media can effect change. By accurately depicting the later years as a time to be enjoyed—a time of spiritual and emotional enrichment with a balance of work and recreation, loss and gain, giving and receiving—the media can

- Enhance the self-esteem and self-confidence of older people, who will see themselves as the respected persons they have a right to be, instead of the "jokes" they are made to seem.
- Help younger people overcome their dread of old age by showing what it is really like and not the fear-filled picture we have of illness and loneliness.
- Help draw generations closer so that younger people recognize their need for older people and vice versa.
- Help resolve serious problems by defining them so they can be addressed.

Children

Ours is a society that claims to love children, but we don't always see them in the media as truly lovable. We are shown the extremes: children either as pampered cherubs or as problems from the moment they are born.

Idealized children are always sweet, clean, healthy, well-dressed, and have only one emotion: radiant joy. They have secure homes with loving, indulgent parents. Babies coo but never cry. Older children are commercial models of prettiness and handsomeness. Curls bounce. Even when a tooth is unavoidably missing, the child is cute.

These plastic-doll children are presented unrealistically, as if they were little adults doing everything grown-up on a smaller scale. Their humor is limited to jokes about the food they eat, and their intelligence is applied only to the toys with which they play.

At the other extreme is the rash of "problem stories" about how much children cost, how they get into all kinds of trouble, and how they create havoc for parents, teachers, authorities, and society in general.

We begin to believe all children have learning, drug, or health problems because that's all we read about and see. Many books and plays cast a child in the role of an agent of evil, able to destroy whole families and communities. Their threatening faces glare at us from the paperback racks. We may even fear them.

Children are, in fact, children—persons with feelings and minds. Children need media treatment that helps them be understood and appreciated until they become adults and can manage their own lives. The following guidelines are intended to support communicators in treating them with dignity and respect in a balanced, unbiased way.

Labels

Designate age only when relevant.

Because the word "children" spans ages of enormous growth and development (a child of 3 is not comparable to a child of 10), knowing the exact age of a child is often helpful to your audience. This practice, however, need not be a ritual when age is irrelevant.

When writing about an age group (sixth graders, for example), specifying individual ages isn't necessary, especially if most are 11 and 12, but John is 14. Children have no set rate of learning, and John should not be singled out as unusual by giving his age. For example:

NO	YES
John Smith, 14, is in the sixth grade.	John Smith is in the sixth grade.

Use accurate terms for age groups.

Acceptable terms are as follows:

- Infant—commonly defined as newborn to age 2.
- Toddler—approximately age 1 to 2 when the child is learning to crawl and walk.
- Preschooler—age 2 to 5.
- Youngster—preschool to about 13.
- Very young child—usually about 5.
- Adolescent—no specific ages but generally the teen years.
- Youth—any age below adulthood (generally 18); sometimes reserved for older adolescents to age 21.

"Teenager" has become associated with the difficulties of adolescence. Consider these substitutes: "young person," "young man," "young woman," "young people." Refer to "the teen years," if you like, instead of "adolescence." Adolescence, however, is not a specific span of years, and it varies with each child, indicating the time from onset of puberty to physical maturity.

Use the young person's name and age, rather than "the teenager" or "the adolescent," since these words are not totally descriptive but represent just one aspect—age—of a person's life.

"Juvenile" is closely associated with "juvenile delinquent," another term with a negative image. It is improperly applied to every child in trouble with the law, although only 5 percent of those incarcerated have actually committed crimes.[19] For this group, "youthful offender" is more accurate; reserve "juvenile delinquent" for those actually convicted of crimes.

Most children who are incarcerated (70 to 80 percent) have been truant from school or have run away from home. Don't label them "truants" or "runaways," but describe their actions, as was done in the previous sentence. Examples of these suggestions:

NO	YES
Teenager, adolescent	Young person, young man, young woman, the teen years
The teenager, the adolescent	Marie Jones, a 16-year-old student . . . .
Juvenile delinquent	Youthful offender
Truants, runaways	Young people who have been truant from school or run away from home

Use positive descriptive words for children.

"Kids" is commonly used as an alternative to "children." Once considered slang, it is

[19]Robert Clampitt, ed., Children's Express, syndicated column, November 10, 1980.

acceptable for informal communication.

"Brats," "retards" (slang implying developmentally impaired, but used generally), "little crooks," "little devils," and "dummies" are part of a litany of damaging words that should not be used by sensitive communicators. They verbally abuse and belittle children and should not be reinforced by continued use. Neither are children "little angels," which implies that they are perfect.

While children are growing up, they learn by trial and error and by example from adults. Labeling them "bad" isn't fair. The headline, "Bad Kids Yield to Peer Pressure and Drink," should rightly read, "Adults Supply Alcohol and Poor Examples to Vulnerable Kids." Similarly, a newspaper indicted all children with the headline, "Romper Room Junkies," when an 8-year-old boy was tragically addicted to heroin by his drug-dealing surrogate father.

Dishonesty is wrong; criminal acts are wrong; drugs are harmful. We must be blunt about saying so. But we don't have to label and condemn with poorly chosen words the children who get trapped in such activities.

Avoid labels that attach a stigma to situations involving children.

Instead of being viewed sympathetically, children of divorced parents are often portrayed as troublemakers who might very well break up a second marriage by not getting along with the new spouse. These children usually assume blame erroneously to begin with. They do not need the added blame of our stigmatizing words.

Stories about single, pregnant young women often fail to address the men involved. The double standard of blaming the female still prevails.

We know statistically that fewer jobs are available for young people than in past generations. However, when they are out of work, they are often described as "shiftless," "lazy," or "spoiled."

Correct these negative impressions by such positive stories as

- Children of divorce who have organized self-help groups.
- Junior Achievement and other programs that provide work experience and advice.
- Organizations that give workshops for students and offer job-search services.

Myths

Show young people positively.

No "problem" children exist—only children with problems. These stories should not be avoided or glossed over. However, more positive stories can convey their talents, accomplishments, heroism, serious goals, and opinions.

Many children are unjustifiably incarcerated or kept in inhumane institutions. Many are the victims of crimes—rape, incest, and murder (2,000 each year in the United States are killed by parents; 1 million injured). Child abuse (sexual, physical, and psychological) is epidemic and growing at a rate of 15 to 20 percent each year. And suicide is a leading cause of death for ages 15 to 24.[20]

These stories and many others must be told in a positive way to inspire solutions. For example:

- Parents Anonymous, a national self-help

[20]*The Detroit News*, May 16, 1978, p. D-1.

group that cures many parents of child-abuse problems.
- Suicide-prevention efforts that help families recognize signs of danger and improve communication.

The sensitive communicator also has many opportunities to help the public understand the slow learner and the gifted child. Research is finding remedies for childhood conditions once considered impossible to alter. These stories need to be told.

Recognize children's self-reliance and citizenship.

Children are not totally dependent. They can cook and sew for themselves, travel alone, study far from home, win awards and scholarships, and often be more self-reliant than adults expect. They are adventurous and daring and have been known to be successful entrepreneurs while still in their teen years. Some even live alone and are self-supporting when they are only 14 or 15.

Communicate such self-reliance, as well as children's talents and helpfulness to others. Art shows, science fairs, and plays put on by youngsters make positive stories. So do the many projects in which children help others. For example:

- Children who participate in walkathons and similar activities to aid charities.
- Children who devise their own fund-raising events for worthy causes.
- 4-H Club awards for crafts, animal husbandry, and so forth.

Sensitive communication can reinforce the fact

that most young people are highly motivated to help themselves and to make positive contributions to the community.

Reflect the variety of appearance of children.

As described earlier, children do not all look alike. They are many shapes, sizes, and colors—not all fashion models.

Childhood is a time of "corrections," including glasses, braces, and special shoes. Children with disabilities wear helmets, walk with crutches, and get about in wheelchairs. Girls are sometimes taller than boys. Boys are not always messy, and girls are not always neat.

Reflect this variety of appearance when you show children. Allow them to be as they are. Focus less on how they look and more on what they do.

Many children have serious illnesses. A sensitive presentation can inform the public about and inspire donations to research and treatment. The line between use and abuse, however, is fine. To avoid exploiting such children, present their stories accurately and recognize the general high level of health of most North American children.

Examples of positive stories:

- Children of various races and abilities on a television program, interacting in natural, everyday situations.
- The girl with glasses engaged in active sports.
- The "poster boy" with healthy siblings or friends who join in his appeal for funds.

For more guidance in depicting children, see Chapter 6.

Portray children according to nonsexist guidelines.

Forget blue for baby boys and pink for baby girls.

Girls play baseball and operate toy trains. Boys play with dolls and cry when hurt. Laws in the United States assure girls as full a sports program at school as boys. Boys take classes in cooking and child care. Girls are leaders as often as boys. They are as competitive and they, too, are being groomed for careers.

Show activities that are not limited by sex-role stereotypes. Show sex-integrated relationships (boys don't play exclusively with boys or girls with girls). Show boys and girls relating to each parent and grandparent, not merely to adults of the same sex. Present children in clothing ads in natural situations, not in the sexy poses of adults.

Reality

Show realistic families and homes.

Few families are now "traditional": mother-father-child; father working and mother staying at home. The reality for most children is quite different.

Many children live with one parent or with a parent and a second (or subsequent) spouse. Some live with relatives, in foster homes, adoptive homes, or institutions. Others live in "extended families" with a mixture of relatives or friends. One out of every five American children today can expect to live with only one parent at some time.[21]

---

[21]U.S. Bureau of the Census, *Daytime Care of Children*, Current Population Reports Series P-20, No. 298 (Washington: Government Printing Office, October, 1976).

Children live in all parts of the country and all kinds of homes—from apartments to farms, from remote cabins to the inner-city. They do a lot of moving around and must make friends and attend new schools on a frequent basis.

Show children in the varied situations they may experience as realities. Change is difficult for all of us, but especially for the child who has seen only a narrow view of life. Some positive stories to do:

- The single mother or father and child having good times together.
- Two mothers and their children who work a farm.
- A newspaper series on children considered hard to adopt who need homes.

Encompass the diversity of ethnic, cultural, and economic backgrounds of children. Young people new to a country are not "culturally deprived" (see Chapter 1) because they speak a different language from the majority. Show their cultural richness. Some children grow up in wealthy families; present their situations, as well as those in poor homes.

Another reality in today's family is that of the working mother. With a majority of all women in the labor force, the number of working mothers is greater than that of those in the home full-time. Traditional roles, then, are gone or blurred. Other people now assist in the care of children—fathers, grandparents, other relatives, hired help.

Since day-care centers in the United States can accommodate only 1 million preschoolers of working parents, some 2.1 million aged 3 to 13 are left with older siblings or people in the home.

Another 1.8 million aged 7 to 13 care for themselves after school and summers.[22]

Communicators can recognize these changes in child care by positive stories:

- A company that provides day care at work for children of employees.
- Neighborhood parents who organize a low-cost, cooperative nursery.

Present child-rearing fairly and realistically.

Children are not always happy, obedient, and tidy. Neither are they always sassy, angry, messy, or depressed. Romanticizing about them as such does a grave disservice and limits them to one dimension.

Parents who seek guidance in child-rearing but hear and read only advice that blames and scolds them feel even more helpless. A realistic, balanced presentation of parent/child issues includes failures, as well as successes. Raising children is hard work, and that fact needs to be communicated—along with the fact that it can also be one of the great joys in life.

Patronizing

Name children only when doing so will not harm them.

Laws prevent the use of names when minors are arrested or are the victims of sexual assaults. A law should also protect children from writers of

---

[22]Seth Low and Pearl Spindler, *Child-Care Arrangements of Working Mothers in the United States* (Washington: Children's Bureau and Women's Bureau, U.S. Department of Labor, 1968).

such stories as the "town thief," in which a 7-year-old girl's name was given. A cartoon showed her running away from a windowsill with a pie, and the story about the small items she stole was written as humor. It wasn't funny to her as she faced living down the cruel experience.

When communicating about children in treatment programs, protect them by not using names, as a general rule. Parents and authorities are often happy to have a child's name and photograph used, however, when an inspiring story is done in a dignified way to encourage others with similar needs. Always ask and get signed permission for any photograph used.

,An example of a positive story using names is one about a piano teacher with a special gift for teaching children with disabilities. Emphasis on their genuine talents and the nonpatronizing tone of the writing made the children proud to have their names mentioned.

Let children speak for themselves.

Too few communicators listen to children or take their comments seriously. One group making itself heard is Children's Express, young reporters who publish a syndicated column of interviews with world leaders and celebrities. In their book, *Listen to Us!*, they prove they can speak quite well about school, family, drugs, sex, being molested, incest, money, television, religion, and other topics.[23]

Their words illustrate that children can be effective communicators. Avoid patronizing when you feature them in stories. Ask them what *they*

---

[23]Children's Express, *Listen to Us!* (New York: Workman Publishing Co., 1978).

think, rather than limiting your sources to the adults involved.

SUMMARY

Older People

1. Designate age only when relevant.
2. Use terms other than "senior citizen"; ask groups or individuals what they prefer to be called.
3. Use words that accurately describe older people.
4. Don't be amazed at the endurance of older people.
5. Recognize that older persons are individuals.
6. Reflect the variety of appearance of older people.
7. Stress that age doesn't necessarily bring loneliness and an end to sexual interest.
8. Present age fairly and realistically.
9. Tell the true health story of older people.
10. Be especially sensitive to the needs of older women.
11. Use words that do not patronize or demean older people.
12. Recognize that older people are not "old babies."
13. Include older persons in mainstream stories.
14. Include employed older persons in stories.
15. Stress action and involvement of older people.

Children

1. Designate age only when relevant.
2. Use accurate terms for age groups.
3. Use positive descriptive words for children.
4. Avoid labels that attach a stigma to situations involving children.
5. Show young people positively.
6. Recognize children's self-reliance and citizenship.
7. Reflect the variety of appearance of children.
8. Portray children according to nonsexist guidelines.
9. Show realistic families and homes.
10. Present child-rearing fairly and realistically.
11. Name children only when doing so will not harm them.
12. Let children speak for themselves.

Chapter 4

Regardless of Disability: Toward Communication Sensitive to Ability

by Lester R. Potter, ABC[1]

"Crippled Computer Operator Still Enjoys Roller Disco"

The communicator with even a dash of professionalism and sensitivity would recoil at the use of such a headline. But all too frequently, disabled people are subjected to just this sort of media treatment.

Sensitivity to people with disabilities should be an integral part of communication in its many forms. Common sense and propriety dictate intuitive guidelines, but heightened awareness is needed as disabled people become more visible in the workforce and other areas of our society. Such

[1]Judy E. Pickens, ABC, communication consultant in Seattle, contributed this chapter in the first edition.

sensitivity must start with an understanding of terms.

Labels

Recognize that "disability" and "handicap" do not mean the same thing.

"Disability" refers to physical, mental, sensory, and emotional impairments that interfere with major tasks of daily living. The most common image of disability is a physical one. But the word encompasses more. Some 36 million Americans have limited physical, mental, and emotional disabilities—one out of every six.[2] One person out of every 10 worldwide has difficulty hearing, seeing, moving, learning, controlling emotions, or talking. That proportion represents approximately 400 million people.[3]

A "typical" disabled person doesn't exist, nor does a psychology of disability, as such, because disabilities produce no firm, predictable effects.

"Handicap" denotes an interaction between a disability and an environment that erects obstacles or barriers to disabled people. The U.S. Vocational Rehabilitation Act of 1973 defines someone with a handicap as "any person who has a physical or mental impairment that substantially limits one or more major life activities, has a record of such an impairment, or is regarded as having such an impairment."[4]

---

[2]Frank Bowe, *Handicapping America: Barriers to Disabled People* (New York: Harper & Row, 1978), p. vii.
[3]Lilly Bruck, *Access: The Guide to a Better Life for Disabled Americans* (New York: Random House, 1978), p. 241.
[4]Cyril M. Rappaport, "Hiring the Handicapped," *Personnel Administrator,* XXV (November, 1980), 86–87.

A "disabled" person need not be "handicapped." A disability can be a handicap in a specific situation. For example, a wheelchair user may have only a *disability* in the home or customary workplace because the condition isn't limiting there, but have a *handicap* in an airport with no ramps or elevators. Examples of how these two words should be properly used are as follows:

NO	YES
He has a handicap that's hardly noticeable.	He has a disability that's hardly noticeable.
We need to recognize on-the-job barriers for handicapped workers.	We need to recognize barriers for disabled workers that can handicap them on the job.

When choosing which word to use, consider the nature of the disability and how the person relates to the environment.

Affirmative Action

Review the legal aspects of communicating with and about disabled people.

While opportunities to communicate with and about disabled persons may arise during the normal workday, communicators very often are *required* to do so as part of an affirmative-action program. As detailed in Chapter 11, both Canadian and United States lawmakers have mandated such communication in relation to physical and mental ability. Review that information and get advice from your affirmative-action coordinator, personnel director, or legal counsel.

Beyond supporting the right to work, sensitive communication can develop an awareness that helps create more opportunities for persons with disabilities and improves their acceptance by coworkers. Seeing disabled people do their jobs effectively takes them out of the realm of oddities and smooths the way to more and better work options.

Stereotypes

Develop a bias-free attitude toward disabled people.

Given the varied nature of disability, no complete list of examples can be practically developed that will steer the communicator through every circumstance. Your personal judgment must frequently be your guide. At the heart of that judgment is your attitude.

That attitude toward disabilities might range from fear, ignorance, and loathing to optimism and solicitude. Articles about over-achieving "super-cripples" are applauded by those who share an attitude of curiosity or who think that disabilities should be glossed over as if they don't exist. The fictitious headline introducing this chapter is, perhaps, a bit exaggerated, but not far off-base as an illustration of what often results from such attitudes. In reality, these attitudes frequently create barriers for disabled people—architectural, educational, occupational, legal, and personal.

In developing a sensitive, positive attitude and making communication judgments based on it, remember that most disabled people are concerned with what the majority takes for granted. They want to get on and off a bus or subway, to enter and exit a building, to attend school, to take full part in their communities, and to live independent lives with dignity.

Consider these examples in which underlying negative messages are corrected:

NO	YES
Story about an epileptic sales manager who travels seven states.	Examine your premise. Imagine doing a story on a sales manager *without* epilepsy who travels seven states. Would you have a story?
Article on a blind person who performs a function characteristically done by sighted people.	Communicate about such situations if you can show how opportunities are developed so that disabilities don't become handicaps. Don't do the article merely to point out that the person is blind.

Stress ability, rather than disability.

Communication that is sensitive to disability respects a disabled person's desire to lead as independent a life as possible. Attitudes toward disability too often are concerned with the concept of "differentness." Communicators can soften the harsh division into "us" and "them" by helping integrate disabled people into the mainstream based on their similarities, rather than segregate them based on their differences.

Avoid mentioning disability when it is not pertinent to the story. Include a disability and the adjustments necessary to overcome it when it is pertinent, but help your audience see the whole person, not just the disability, by showing limitations in an unobtrusive manner. For example:

NO	YES
The deaf accountant spotted the error.	The accountant spotted the error.
The promotion has helped expand his career potential. But what makes John different from other recently promoted employees is that he is blind.	John, overcoming blindness, has earned a promotion that helps expand his career potential. *or* John has earned a promotion that helps expand his career potential.
The handicapped parents met to exchange ideas.	The parents, each with some disability, met to exchange ideas.
An epileptic, Mary has no trouble doing her job.	Mary's epilepsy has no effect on her job performance.
Fill out the form, then take it to the clerk in the wheelchair.	Fill out the form, then take it to the second clerk from the left.

Another example of positive treatment is the television series, "Ironside," about a paraplegic police detective. The series downplayed his disability and focused on his activities and achievements.

Measure disabled people against their own criteria, not so-called "normal" ability.

In communicating with and about those with disabilities, the tendency is to depict them trying to perform close to what society holds as normal, competing according to the same set of rules that apply to nondisabled people. Wheelchair marathoners and blind typists are among the subjects that approach cliché status.

Do not communicate with and about a disabled person in terms of functioning almost as "normal." Such treatment presupposes that 100-percent physical or mental ability is normal. An amputee may not play basketball or want to, but may be exemplary in job performance. The differences are real, but so are the abilities of each person.

Look at *actual* ability, not at *comparative* ability, because disabled people have the right to be communicated with and about in a fair and equitable manner—according to rules that apply to them. Avoid comparative statements that imply they don't quite measure up. For example:

NO	YES
Though paralyzed, she gets around almost as well as other customer-service personnel.	She performs her duties like other customer-service personnel and gets around the large sales area very well.
At the company picnic, Sally, an amputee, played volleyball almost as well as healthy employees.	At the company picnic, Sally helped the Blue Team win the trophy. *or* At the company picnic, Sally held her own in the volleyball tournament, helping the Blue Team win.

Henry, though deaf, is an excellent auditor and understands complex requirements of auditing as well as employees who can hear.	Henry's hearing impairment has proven to be no handicap in managing the complex requirements of his role in operations auditing.
We have found that people confined to wheelchairs can fill orders almost as fast as clerks who can walk.	Given the size and layout of the warehouse, clerks who are wheelchair users perform competitively.
Though both are deaf, they are an incredibly intelligent couple.	They are an incredibly intelligent couple.

Avoid using adjectives as nouns and unfairly limiting disabled people.

Very often, people with disabilities are grouped and referred to as "the deaf," "the blind," and "the mentally ill." This practice presupposes that everyone who is deaf, blind, or mentally ill is identical. Using adjectives as nouns conspicuously deletes the humanizing that occurs when "people," "person," "individual," or similar nouns are inserted.

Such usage unfairly groups and labels disabled people, setting them apart from nondisabled people and making the disability their overwhelming attribute. For example:

NO	YES
The deaf, the blind	The woman who is deaf, the man who is blind
The handicapped	People with disabilities or, only if limiting, People with handicaps

Demeaning

Use words and phrases that appropriately describe and do not offend.

Following are examples of words and phrases now generally considered unacceptable and their acceptable alternatives:

NO	YES
Crippled, crip, gimp	Physically limited, motion impaired, disabled *or, specifically,* Paraplegic, quadriplegic, hemiplegic, amputee, cerebral palsied
Confined to a wheelchair	Wheelchair user
Insane, retarded, dull, crazy, half-witted	Mentally or emotionally impaired, learning disabled, slow learner, brain damaged, developmentally disadvantaged, disabled
Deaf and dumb, deaf mute, deaf girl/boy	Hearing or speech impaired, deaf, disabled
Midget, dwarf	Little person, growth impaired
Fits, spells, attacks	Seizures, epilepsy, disabled

Words or expressions frequently used that should be purged from the sensitive communicator's vocabulary are "cripple," "spastic," "retarded," and "dumb" or "mute." Often used lightly, they are as biased as racial slurs and have no place in our language today.

SUMMARY

1. Recognize that "disability" and "handicap" do not mean the same thing.
2. Review the legal aspects of communicating with and about disabled people.
3. Develop a bias-free attitude toward disabled people.
4. Stress ability, rather than disability.
5. Measure disabled people against their own criteria, not so-called "normal" ability.
6. Avoid using adjectives as nouns and unfairly limiting disabled people.
7. Use words and phrases that appropriately describe and do not offend.

PART 2

Applying Bias-Free Principles

Chapter 5

Avoiding Sexism on the Job: A Test for Bias-Free Writing and Speaking

Chapter 6

Bias-Free Visual Media

Chapter 7

Face-to-Face: Eliminating Bias From Meetings

Chapter 5

Avoiding Sexism on the Job: A Test for Bias-Free Writing and Speaking

by Mary Munter[1]

The time has come. Instead of subjective moral pronouncements, we need a perfectly scientific, completely foolproof, highly theoretical model for avoiding sexism on the job—in business, industry, government, the professions, and elsewhere.

---

[1]The author acknowledges the following references that have contributed to this chapter: Loisanne Foerster and Patricia Walsh Rao, "Created Equal: Toward Communication Free of Sexual Bias," in the first edition of this book. Patricia Hogan, "A Woman Is Not a Girl and Other Lessons in Corporate Speech," *Business and Society Review*, No. 14 (Summer, 1975), 34–38. Ruth Lieben, et al. *Salutation Survey* (Honolulu: Country Committee on the Status of Women, 1979). "Addendum to Style Guide for Authors," *Academy of Management Review*, I, No. 3 (1976).

May I suggest for your consideration just such a model: the well-formulated and extensively researched Munter Turnaround Test (MTT). Rules for applying this test are simple: To check for biased thinking (which, of course, expresses itself in biased language), substitute "woman" whenever hoary tradition dictates "man" in writing or speaking.

To illustrate the MTT, I will explain the most prevalent on-the-job sexism problems. For writing, they are (1) generic terms, (2) job titles, (3) value-laden expressions, (4) third-person pronouns, and (5) salutations. For speaking, they are (1) child references, (2) business talk, (3) rough language, (4) sexual innuendo, and (5) secretarial assumptions. In each case, you will note, I have applied the MTT. (For more guidance on avoiding sexism in language, see Chapter 2.)

Writing

Applying the MTT to writing is relatively easy. When you write, you think more carefully than when you speak. You revise and refine. Therefore, you have no excuse for misusing any of the following elements:

Generic Terms

"All women are created equal." Now, don't worry, gentlemen; that word "women" applies to you as well, of course. It's simply traditional to use the word "woman" instead of "man." We can't change the Declaration of Independence, after all.

Correct. However, we certainly *can* change current expressions in writing that suggest that women are the only people on earth. These changes are simple to make. Just remember the plural of "person" is usually "people," not "persons."

NO	YES
The woman on the way up	The executive on the way up
Woman-made	Artificial, synthetic
Woman hours	Staff hours, working hours
Organization women	Organization people
Workwoman's compensation	Worker's compensation

Job Titles

"The directorwomen met with the shareholderwomen yesterday." Now, don't worry, gents; of course, you can be a directorwoman or a shareholderwoman, too. It's just traditional to attach that "woman" suffix to any job you might possibly want.

This offender is, perhaps, the easiest of all to remedy. We simply have no excuse for continuing to use "woman" as a job-title suffix. Some examples:

NO	YES
Businesswoman	Executive, manager
Chairwoman	Chair, moderator
Forewoman	Supervisor
Newswoman	Reporter
Policewoman	Police officer

Saleswoman	Sales representative, sales clerk
Workwoman	Worker, employee

Value-Laden Expressions

"This is a woman-sized job." Of course, we don't mean to imply that a man couldn't do it. It's just that, well, it's such a big *job.*

If it's a big job, call it a big job. Avoid these value judgments based on sex:

NO	YES
A woman-sized job	Sizable, large
A womanly effort	Valiant
Womanpower	Workers, workforce

Third-Person Pronouns

"Each manager must ask herself . . . ." Of course, that includes you men, as well; but you know how it is with language. The subject and the verb must agree. So we'll just always use the feminine, okay?

This offender represents more of a problem to the bias-conscious writer. You have four ways to solve it: (1) reword, (2) recase into the plural, (3) replace pronouns with "one," "you," "he or she," "hers or his," or (4) alternate male and female words. For example:

NO	YES
Typically, a manager will call monthly meetings with her staff.	Typically, a manager will call monthly staff meetings. (Reword.)

Each manager must ask herself	Managers must ask themselves . . . . (Recase.)
Her staff	Her or his staff (Replace.)
The job interview form might include statements such as these: "She's not the right person for the company" or "She lacks the necessary qualifications."	The job interview form might include statements such as these: "She's not the right person for the company" or "He lacks the necessary qualifications." (Alternate.)

Salutations

We teach our boys in typing and secretarial classes to use the salutations "Dear Madams:" or "Ladies:" when the sexual makeup of the readership is unknown. Naturally, that opening includes men, too.

Several alternatives will correct this problem. Unless you elect to omit the salutation altogether, you may choose from these alternatives:

Use a descriptive term.

Dear Customer:
Dear Colleague:
Dear Subscriber:

Use a job title.

Dear Sales Representative:
Dear Permissions Editor:

Use formal asexual salutations.

Dear Recipient:
Dear Sir/Madam:
To Whom It May Concern:

Use informal asexual salutations.

Dear Reader,
Dear Friend(s),
Greetings (or regional variations, such as Howdy or Aloha).

Speaking

What you say aloud, of course, is more spontaneous than what you write. Therefore, you must be especially careful to avoid blatant and subtle bias. Applying the MTT to the most prevalent examples of sexist language in conversation leads to the following results:

Child References

After a two-hour planning meeting, the committee has compiled recommendations for a new policy. The next step is to have them typed up and distributed. One of the members volunteers, "I'll have my boy take care of it."

The term "my boy" is insidious. It implies that men are both dependent children and chattel. Furthermore, it unnecessarily emphasizes their sex (male), rather than their function (clerical).

Business Talk

Four women and two men attend a luncheon meeting. The conversation has been complex and technical as they discuss a new computer system. After an hour, one of the women turns to the two men and asks, "Are we boring you gentlemen with all this business talk?"

Think about the assumptions implicit in that question. It assumes, first, that men are not interested in business matters and, second, that they are merely passive agents (Are *we* boring you?).

Rough Language

The taskforce meets for its final session. The policy decisions have been made; the implementation is about to begin. One woman leans back in her chair and summarizes, "This is going to be a hell of a lot of work. Oh, pardon the language, guys."

Don't assume that all men have the same attitude toward rough language. Some men object to its use; some don't. Judge your audience as individuals, not as a sex group.

Sexual Innuendoes

Bob Wilson's promotion has just been announced. Two women are standing together in the hall when Bob, a good-looking young man, walks by. One nudges and winks, "We all know how he got the promotion."

The comment is another variation on the virgin-and-the-stud dichotomy, which has plagued men throughout history (see the previous discussion on rough language). Again, judge your audience as individuals. Men *can* get ahead because of qualities other than looks.

Secretarial Assumptions

A man is standing near the copy machine. A woman walks up to him and asks, "Excuse me, young man. Are you Ms. Blake's secretary?"

Do not assume that any man within reach of a copy machine, a coffee pot, or a telephone is a secretary. Think of how hard men must try to avoid physical proximity to these objects in any work situation.

SUMMARY

Writing

1. Select generic terms that include both sexes in general references.
2. Use sexually neutral job titles.
3. Choose expressions that do not value one sex over the other.
4. Use alternatives to sex-designating pronouns when referring to both sexes.
5. Neutralize a business letter when sex of the recipient is unknown by omitting a salutation or by using a descriptive term, a job title, or an asexual salutation.

Speaking

1. Refer to adults as adults, not as children.
2. Recognize that members of either sex can be interested in business affairs.

3. Judge your audience as individuals in acceptance of rough language.
4. Avoid sexual innuendoes regarding job advancement.
5. Recognize that neither sex has a monopoly on any specific job.

Chapter 6

Bias-Free Visual Media

by Stewart L. Burge, ABC[1]

"A picture is worth more than ten thousand words."

"Seeing is believing."

These tired, but true, maxims have direct application for communicators who care about the impressions their messages and media make on audiences.

Many of the "thou shalt not's" applicable to visualization of subject matter are identical to those that apply to writing and speaking. For example, a photograph or film footage that is demeaning, insulting, or otherwise denigrating to any person or group is inappropriate, as are demeaning, insulting, or denigrating words. Out of

[1]Judy E. Pickens, ABC, communication consultant in Seattle, contributed this chapter in the first edition.

place, too, are visual media that rely on sexual, racial, or other stereotyping to make a point.

Blatant lack of judgment in such areas, however, seems not to be widespread today. The considerable attention focused in recent years on the desirability of nondiscriminatory communication has done much to increase awareness and sensitivity, at least among professional communicators.

More frequently now, problems develop in those vast, fuzzy areas of communication that are subject to personal interpretation. And, since not everyone's sensitivities are assaulted by the same things, common-sense judgment becomes extremely important in developing effective, unbiased visual communication.

Messages Without Words

Speech isn't always necessary to convey very specific messages to people around you. For instance, what do you "say" by the way you walk, sit, dress, or wear your hair?

The importance of nonverbal messages cannot be ignored. Researchers report that from 65 to more than 90 percent of the messages communicated in a face-to-face encounter are carried on the "nonverbal" band. Further, they tell us, when verbal and nonverbal messages coming from the same person are contradictory, nonverbal messages usually predominate in the interpretation of the person receiving the two sets of information.[2]

---

[2]John Keltner, *Interpersonal Speech Communication* (Belmont: Wadsworth, 1970), p. 38.

These "silent" messages are very much part of photographs, slides, videotapes, and other visuals and must be monitored to be sure they are saying what we want them to say. Nonverbal information must reinforce (rather than contradict) verbal or written information.

One of the surest transmitters of nonverbal messages is the human body—its behavior and appearance. The fascinating study of these various elements is "kinesics" or "body language." A great deal of research in this area can be conveniently grouped into four categories: the face, the general shape of the body, touching, and posture and gesture. Of the four, communicators most often must monitor posture and gesture when evaluating photos, illustrations, and other visuals.

As an example, a study by researcher Albert Mehrabian concluded that people relax most with someone perceived to have a lower status, second-most with a peer, and least with someone perceived to have a higher status than their own.[3]

Mehrabian also found that men remain more tense when with a disliked male than when with a disliked female. Perhaps this finding is evidence of an attitude of male superiority that is fast disappearing in modern organizations and society.

Another nonverbal message is conveyed by territory. An accepted behavior characteristic in most animals (including humans) is to lay claim to and defend particular areas as their own. Studies of this phenomenon conclude that a psychological advantage exists to being in one's own territory,

---

[3]Albert Mehrabian, "Communication Without Words," *Psychology Today*, II (February, 1968), pp. 52–55.

not unlike the "home-field advantage" found in athletic competition.

Three principles relate to territory and personal status in organizations: Persons with higher status will normally have more territory than persons with lower status, protect their territory better, and invade the territory of lower-status persons. Roughly translated, these characteristics mean that the higher a person is in an organization, the more and better space that person will have, the better it will be protected, and the easier that person can move, uninvited, into the territory of lower-ranking employees.[4]

These nonverbal elements of territory and body language are interpreted in visual communication by positioning. The person in the "primary" position is dominant, while the person in the "secondary" position is subordinate. For example, the driver of a car is in the primary and controlling position (unless it's a chauffeur), and the passenger is in the secondary, passive position. When media most often present a male driver and a female passenger, they make a statement about sexual roles and abilities, based on positioning.

Portray persons of comparable status equally.

Do your visual messages depict persons of comparable levels or jobs equally? Do their postures and gestures suggest that they are equally at ease in the situation? Or is one person open and relaxed (indicating authority and dominance), while the other is rigid and motionless (suggesting inferiority and lack of power)?

---

[4]Gerald Goldhaber, *Organizational Communication* (Dubuque: Wm. C. Brown Company, 1974), p. 150.

For example, seeing a man seated at a desk while a woman stands at his side or in front of him signals the viewer that the man is probably dominant in the relationship. To alter this perception, simply show both of them seated or both of them standing (Figures 1 and 2).[5]

Showing the Bigger Picture

Use visuals to help alter stereotypic roles.

Avoid situations that consistently show members of any group as superior or inferior. No matter how subtle, the implication is that people in certain groups *belong* in particular roles, for example, Spanish-surnamed persons when consistently portrayed as blue-collar workers or women as clerical employees (Figures 3, 4, 5, and 6).

Perhaps the most obvious reinforcement of sex-role stereotyping is the treatment of women as pretty, sociable, and shallow. Such sexism often occurs at grand openings and similar occasions when the local beauty queen cuts the ribbon. This type of event and the photos or film footage that results reinforce limited thinking about abilities of women. Begin to change this demeaning practice by convincing planners to ask instead a prominent business executive or other more appropriate person to participate in the opening.

If plans can't be altered, the communicator must, then, work with what is available. When the event falls into the category of cheesecake, consider these options:

---

[5]Illustrations for this chapter courtesy Mead Corporation, Dayton, OH, and J. Curtis Hopkins, Sacramento, CA.

Figure 1. The positions of these two persons imply that the man is dominant and the woman subservient.

Figure 2. The positions of these three persons imply more of a peer relationship.

Figure 3. The woman's race, sex, and job reinforce the image of Blacks as servants and women as care-givers. (Note that *all* the passengers are white men.)

- Ignore it. Such events are set up for publicity and will fade more rapidly if none is given.
- Don't use a photo or footage but mention the woman by name and occupation or school in your account of the event. Save your photo space or air time for other aspects of the opening, for instance, the first customer through the door.

Figure 4. Here a Black man is portrayed in a responsible position on par with (or, perhaps, higher than) the others.

Figure 5. The message here is that women are clerical employees and that men are supervisors; also conveyed is the "woman who got her man" stereotype.

Figure 6. Position, attire, and involvement support the fact that both women and men have diverse occupations and are responsible and cooperative.

- Give the woman some depth by showing her interest in merchandise, for example. Illustrate that she knows how to do something besides cut ribbons.

Cartoons—whether animated or still—easily contribute to biased communication since much humor is still based on sexual and racial stereotypes. The characterization of women as dumb broads with no business sense often appears, as does the characterization of men as inept around the house. Racial or ethnic slurs in cartoon form are also offensive to many people and are quickly becoming unacceptable put-downs for any audience.

The artist who brings life to objects such as machinery or office equipment should keep stereotyping in mind. For example, illustrations that depict the big, fast, sleek car as male and the compact, dumpy, utility model as female aren't fair and can be offensive.

Such cartoons should be avoided and consideration given to substituting others that are still humorous or still meet the communication objective—but that make a positive statement. Wise use of the element of humor can even be a lighthearted, subtle way to discourage stereotyping.

Present a balanced image, over-all.

Following this guideline can be as simple as checking faces in the viewfinder before shooting, carefully selecting footage, or cropping judiciously.

For example, a video news story or slide presentation showing only some of the people working on a project presents the communicator with a choice about which ones to use—and about equal treatment. If all supervisors are men (as is still often the case), the result will be all-male groupings if only the top people are shown. An alternative is to select persons representative of the total "team" and, thereby, balance men and women, races, ages, and abilities, and give recognition to a broader range of individuals who are contributing to the project.

A balance need not be struck in every photograph, slide, or film segment. The total publication, slide presentation, or videotape should be evaluated, as should the organization's entire communication effort for an extended period of time to determine consistency of treatment (Figures 7, 8, and 9).

Don't try so hard not to discriminate that visuals appear staged solely to portray equality. Present an *accurate* image of your organization, but offset white-only stories and photos with material that substantiates the involvement of other races, when such is the case. Only by taking affirmative

Figure 7. Men and women as employees and as customers present a balanced picture.

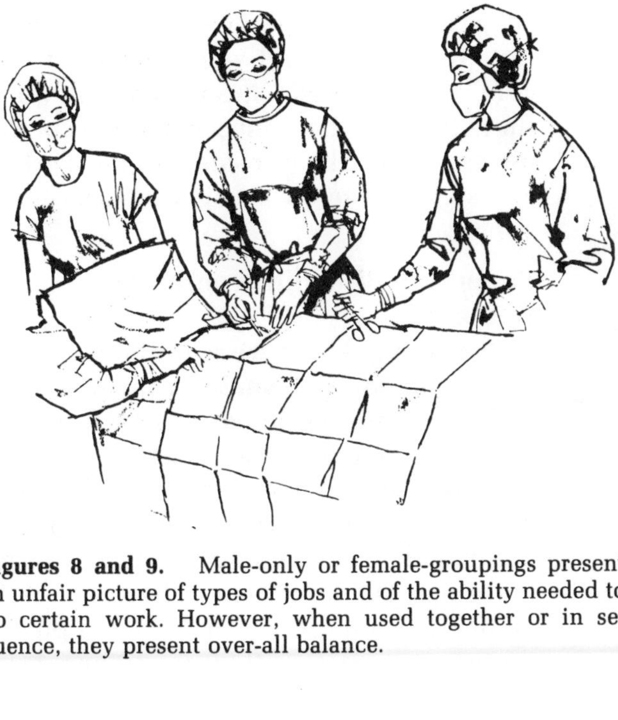

Figures 8 and 9. Male-only or female-groupings present an unfair picture of types of jobs and of the ability needed to do certain work. However, when used together or in sequence, they present over-all balance.

action—by seeking out and including a visual balance of people at a wide range of job levels—can the communicator help improve that makeup by encouraging people to aspire to roles that traditionally have been out of reach.

True to Life

Depict features as they are.

Asian skin is not bright yellow; shades of brown or tan are more realistic. Facial structures vary greatly among Chinese, Japanese, and Koreans. Blacks don't all look alike, either in skin tone or facial structure. Allowing time to research can result in more accurate visual communication.

People are varied in shape and size. Show this diversity, especially when you can hand-pick your subjects. For example, when assembling the cast for a film, don't limit your selection to young, slim, white, athletic specimens with no visible limitations. Rather, select players according to the needs of your film (for salespeople, clerks, drivers, and so forth), not according to some ideal of appearance.

Emphasize disabilities only when relevant.

Similarly, people with disabilities should be shown as they are. Neither camouflage nor highlight a visible impairment but present it in context, when pertinent. For instance, if the story is about a person who uses a wheelchair, include that wheelchair in photos if the emphasis is on reducing barriers on city streets and in public buildings. Don't include it, however, if the emphasis is on that person's role as president of a service organization (Figures 10 and 11). See

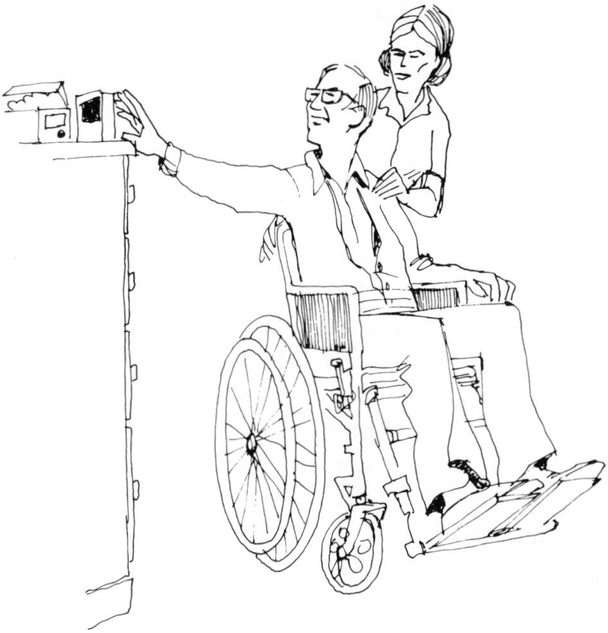

Figure 10. Sensitive portrayal of disabled people does not focus on the disability when irrelevant to the message.

Figure 11. Downplay or ignore a disability by directing the viewer's eye to other features or to an activity.

Chapter 4 for additional guidelines related to disability.

Present realistic images of age.

Keep the following points in mind to depict older people as they are. See Chapter 3 for additional guidelines about age.

- Show realistic scenes and situations but avoid extremes. Show that life isn't all work or all play, all loneliness and nursing homes or all close families, all sedentary days or all a whirl of activity, all poverty or all well-financed leisure (Figures 12 and 13).
- Integrate ages in visuals, showing older people with more than contemporaries or little children.
- Depict a variety of physical appearance (including skin folds and other characteristics that distinguish age) and the contemporary dress of most older people.
- Take special pains to show older women as attractively as possible to compensate for society's harsh judgments of them. (Older men

Figure 12. A distorted picture of older people is conveyed when they are consistently portrayed as ill and sedentary.

Figure 13. By showing a variety of appearance and activities the communicator presents a more realistic view.

have "character," while older women are "hags.") Shoot and crop to avoid emphasizing extra weight or stooped shoulders that might embarrass your subjects.

- Don't stereotype older people as lacking in affection for others or as sexless.
- Avoid stereotyping older people (especially in commercials and films) as bossy, crabby, outspoken, scatterbrained, hard of hearing, and in need of guidance from patronizing younger people.
- Show more older women than older men in proportion to their representation in the population, in a variety of settings, and doing more than domestic activities.
- Do not gloss over or avoid showing the rigors

Figure 14. Such a "Father Knows Best" image of the family is both inaccurate for the majority of North Americans and unfairly limiting by its use of role stereotypes.

of years but use such visuals to call attention to problems that need solutions.

Keep these points in mind to depict children as they are:

- Don't portray all children as well-behaved fashion models, but reflect their variety of emotion and appearance.
- Depict children interacting with their peers and with adults of both sexes.
- Show realistic homes and families in various settings and economic conditions; don't reinforce the "traditional" family as the norm (Figures 14 and 15).

Adhere to nondiscriminatory writing principles in cutlines, scripts, and other language associated with visual media, as set forth elsewhere in this book.

Figure 15. This family makeup is a reality for many children, and showing it helps present a more accurate picture.

SUMMARY

1. Portray persons of comparable status equally.
2. Use visuals to help alter stereotypic roles.
3. Present a balanced image, over-all.
4. Depict features as they are.
5. Emphasize disabilities only when relevant.
6. Present realistic images of age.
7. Adhere to nondiscriminatory writing principles in cutlines, scripts, and other language associated with visual media, as set forth elsewhere in this book.

Chapter 7

Face-to-Face: Eliminating Bias From Meetings

by Linda Cook Roberts

Organizations that espouse equal opportunity and unbiased communication often plan, publicize, and conduct meetings that ignore these principles.

Business meetings, professional-association meetings, luncheons, conferences, taskforce sessions, board meetings, town meetings, conventions, workshops, chapter meetings, training classes, staff meetings, annual conferences, and annual meetings—the list seems endless. An estimated 11 *million* meetings of all kinds are conducted every day in the United States alone. By sheer numbers, then, meetings are a potentially powerful medium in which to reinforce—or undermine—equal opportunity.

Meetings are stages on which bias is often subtly acted out. In perhaps no other setting might a communicator consciously use sexual or racial jokes "all in fun." In no other circumstance might a communicator proceed without carefully considering the entire audience.

No other medium offers more variety, uses more modes of communication, or relies upon more types of media than meetings. These media include written, visual, audiovisual, verbal, and nonverbal. Each may take a variety of forms, for example:

- Written—news releases, meeting guides, and training materials.
- Verbal—speeches, announcements, and presentations.
- Visual and audiovisual—flip charts, films, slide shows, videotapes, and all types of entertainment.

The latter category is of growing importance because of increased preference for visual media in our culture. This trend is especially apparent in audiences of blue-collar workers and young people in all types of jobs. More than a generation of North Americans have been reared to prefer television, films, and other audiovisual media to the printed word as means of receiving information from their organizations.

Information that in the past was presented exclusively in written form (such as a year-end summary or promotion for a new sales campaign) is now being dispensed at meetings via films, tape/slide shows, and the like. Because of the insidious nature of visual media—their enhanced ability to convey and reinforce a message—today's communicator must be especially attentive to keep bias out of these materials. See Chapter 6 for additional guidelines related to visuals.

One other element makes meetings an important place to communicate without bias: the human element. Unlike a magazine or television story, the communicator in meetings is face-to-face with others who may be painfully offended by biased communication.

The following examples show how bias may affect meetings specifically, and guidelines offer direction to avoid these errors.

Planning

Communication and public-relations personnel (as well as executives, managers, and other "nonprofessional" communicators) are frequently called upon to help arrange meetings for their employers or professional groups. Among planning considerations are making job assignments, picking the meeting facility, and timing the schedule.

Select meeting assistants based on ability, not on role stereotypes.

When choosing members of a hospitality committee or assigning other duties, planners often fall back on seemingly harmless role stereotypes. This lapse can have unplanned results, for example:

The moderator of a firm's annual meeting stepped forward to rebut a questioner who had asked about the company's practices in hiring and promoting women. "Of course we have many fine female employees–just look here!" he blustered, dramatically gesturing toward the back of the room. There were members of the all-female hospitality committee, attired alike in aproned hostess dresses.

Do not pick meeting assistants on the basis of looks in order to "dress up" the occasion. When a planner automatically selects only "attractive" young women to act as hostesses, the statement is made that women are decorative. This stereotyping is detrimental to the morale of some participants and to the internal and external image of the organization.

Select a mixture of male, female, younger, and older helpers who are able to do the jobs. Be sure that their attire is business-like and not calculated to call attention to physical attributes.

Organizers also may automatically assume that the roles of food-planner, note-taker, and so on naturally belong to females, even when the meeting is being arranged and attended by both male and female peers. This assumption suggests that the role of supplier of coffee and nametags ("care-giver") is appropriate for (and, apparently, exclusive to) women.

Having willingly agreed to serve on a particular church board because its area of responsibility was of special interest, the woman enthusiastically attended the next meeting, only to be asked to take minutes. "I was the only woman there," she recalled. "I'm a teacher; I don't know how to type so I wasn't asked because of any skill. I was asked because I'm a woman."

Request meeting assistance according to ability, not such role stereotypes.

Select readers and speakers who represent a cross-section of the organization.

The way program participants are selected also can compromise affirmative-action principles:

A Black man who was attending a conference of a professional organization observed, "We have more than 50 percent female and 20 percent minority-group members. Where are the female and minority-group workshop leaders?"

Just as in hiring patterns, selection of speakers and workshop leaders can reflect an unconscious bias or blindspot that is inconsistent with the intent of an organization's equal-opportunity policy.

Speakers and leaders should, first of all, be competent to do the job. Second, they should be representative of the makeup of the organization and the meeting audience. Take affirmative action and bring women and members of minority groups out from behind the scenes, involve a mixture of ages, and don't be embarrassed to put a disabled person on the speaker's platform.

To do so requires a conscious effort at planning the agenda. Try to balance each level of involvement (main speakers and workshop leaders, convenors and recorders) so that no one group has all the "really important" assignments. Plan backups if you can so that, if someone falls through, you can preserve your hard-earned balance.

Plan meeting facilities and schedules so that people with disabilities can participate fully.

Because affirmative-action programs have helped clear the way for more disabled people in the work-place and because disabled people are active in many types of organizations that conduct meetings, planners must take their needs into account when arranging facilities and schedules.

Wheelchair users should be able to get into meeting rooms and position themselves to be involved in discussions, not be relegated to a back corner. They should have adequate room so they don't have to inconvenience other participants or block aisles or exits, two frequent occurrences that are embarrassing to wheelchair users and imply that they are imposing or that their presence is a nuisance.

People with hearing or sight limitations should be granted the privilege of the front of the room. Participants who use crutches or other mobility assistance should not have to struggle to the middle of a row of seats.

All facilities—meeting rooms, dining rooms, restrooms, hallways, and even the parking lot—should be accessible to people with disabilities. Modify the banquet dais or speaker's platform to be fully usable by a disabled speaker or award recipient and to avoid depriving the audience of seeing that person or hearing the speech, especially if the person is using a wheelchair.

Your advanced-registration form can help you plan. Include a line such as "We want to make sure that everyone can participate fully in the conference. Do you have any physical limitation for which we should plan? If so, what?" Then work with the site coordinator to make sure stated needs are adequately and conveniently met. You may even want to check out airports and bus terminals where disabled participants will arrive to anticipate any difficulties they might have getting to the meeting location.

Plan the meeting schedule so that people with limited mobility do not miss part of what they came for because insufficient time was allowed between sessions to switch rooms. A fully mobile person might be able to traverse from one end of a hotel to the other in five minutes flat to keep a tight schedule of workshop sessions; someone using a walker would be left out.

Publicity

Depict people in meeting publicity in ways that are not stereotyping or demeaning.

Publicizing business or professional meetings is also the communicator's responsibility. As affirmative-action objectives are achieved, the makeup of companies and other organizations is changing to include more and more women and minority-group members. In turn, these employees are joining professional associations in their fields. Yet the writers of promotional materials for business, sales, training, and association meetings often apparently are unaware of their audiences. Here are some results:

The sales representative, a woman, received a meeting announcement picturing a voluptuous bikini-clad model lying across a carton of the company's product. The copy purred, "Don't miss the sales roundup–we'll really make it worth your while . . . ."

A training coordinator for a large bank was searching for a workshop suitable for first-line supervisors, many of whom were female and minority employees. "One brochure after another depicted all supervisors as white males," he recalled. "Department heads say the supervisors have begun to grumble about that sort of thing. I couldn't find a program that would sell, based on the literature."

The flier proclaimed, "Get out of your rocker and come to the March meeting!" Accompanying artwork showed a feeble, gray-haired woman in a dark, shapeless dress, seated in a rocking chair knitting. "I didn't go," explained one member in his 60s. "I didn't appreciate the implication that all older people are so sedentary. I told them I was too busy!"

The incentive for people to attend a meeting—or their ability to identify with its subject matter—is lessened when publicity (fliers, brochures, posters, and other advance materials) depicts them in a stereotyped or demeaning manner, or ignores them completely. As a result, a communicator risks losing a segment of the audience.

In addition, organizations whose communicators depict women as sex objects, or stereotype other groups, contradict their equal-opportunity positions and lose credibility with employees, government compliance agencies, and the public.

Conducting the Meeting

Bias also can be reflected in the meeting itself—in introductions, entertainment, visuals, and in written and spoken materials.

Introducing Speakers

Introduce speakers without alluding to sex, physical attributes, or other irrelevant qualities.

Stick to business. Introductions can have a critical impact on the acceptance of the person introduced. That person's effectiveness or authority in the group may be diminished by irrelevant or trivial remarks that, for example, reduce the recipient to an object of sexual interest:

"Judy, don't get me wrong," the club president quipped while eyeing the woman with obvious physical appreciation, "but I sure have a rough time introducing you as chairman!"

Selecting Entertainment and Visual Aids

Design meeting entertainment and visuals so that they are not stereotyping or demeaning.

The opening extravaganza for a convention, professional entertainment at a banquet, and guest program are other areas where the conscientious communicator has an opportunity to support equal treatment. The opposite result is still all too common:

A woman who led her company in sales one year was invited to speak at the annual sales meeting. She was scheduled to appear after the entertainment. To her embarrassment, she found herself on stage following a "sales-boosting" show featuring skantily clad female dancers. "I looked out across the lights," she reported, "and wondered how I could be taken seriously in the face of this blatant display of women as decorations and attention-getters. I wondered how the women in the audience might be feeling."

"What kind of 'guest' program is this?" questioned the husband of a conferee. Advance materials hadn't detailed the agenda but had promised "three exciting days in and around Montreal." What he found was a dreary series of luncheons, fashion shows, and garden tours. "I wasn't the only one to complain," he stated. "Even many of the women didn't appreciate the assumptions about who 'guests' are or what women's interests are."

Eliminating the "girlie" approach to a meeting's visuals or entertainment may mean overcoming long-standing tradition. Meeting organizers have looked to the entertainment world for examples, but the typical variety show is out of place in today's organizations. What went over in the smoker atmosphere no longer will, now that women and members of minority groups are joining the club.

Equally important, slides, films, videotapes, charts, and other visuals are ineffective when they are unappealing or (worse yet) when they are offensive to a segment of the audience. Visual aids that use women to add "interest" also place an extra and unnecessary burden on women who deserve to be taken seriously in an organization:

A senior executive was in charge of his unit's yearly meeting for managers, many of whom were women. In the midst of his slide presentation, a three-quarter, rear view of a shapely woman suddenly appeared, clad only in a t-shirt emblazoned with the company's logo. This slide, the executive snickered, illustrated his point about "the bottom line."

Such treatment goes beyond a lapse of taste. It is indicative of something fundamentally missing from that manager's understanding of the relationship between demeaning sexual treatment and the success of the organization, between "harmless fun" and the severe embarrassment and damaged morale of the professional women present.

Similarly, imagine the reaction of the organization's Black middle managers if the slide had, instead, depicted a vaudeville Black in "white face." If this example seems archaic and out-of-the question, think for a moment about why, in many organizations, sexually stereotyped treatment is still condoned as harmless.

Viewers more likely will be interested when meeting visuals include characters, models, or illustrated figures to which they can relate. Visuals can range from casting a film to preparing stick figures for a chart. For example:

NO	YES
All-male figures on a graph depicting growth in assembly-line employment and all-female figures depicting increases in clerical workers.	Use figures of both sexes in each category. Reflect affirmative-action achievements by proportioning male and female figures in relation to the actual mix in the workforce.

A company film that includes a young woman as a caterpillar operator to stimulate "interest," while presenting all other women and men in stereotypic roles.	Avoid offending any one group subtly by mixing sexes, races, ages, and abilities in a variety of believable roles throughout the film.
Use of a segment from a silent movie showing a Black as a bumbling servant to a white family.	Reevaluate the objective. It may be appropriate for a meeting of sociologists or film historians—but not as entertainment for engineers.
Interviewers in a company video program that are all young and "good looking."	Present a mixture of ages; emphasize ability to interview, not appearance.

The Spoken Word

Consider the composition of the audience when preparing speeches and supporting materials.

Guidelines suggested throughout this book apply here, also, because the spoken word often carries unintended messages in meetings:

For three days, several hundred conference goers moved earnestly from one workshop to another. They heard, "The speaker keeps his *audience by using interest-attracting tricks." "You need feedback as much as the next* fellow*." "When presenting proposals to your boss, keep one thing foremost in your mind:* his *budget." "You're professionals; the* guy *who recognizes that fact is one step ahead of the game." The meeting: an annual conference of communication specialists, of whom half were women.*

Stop such bias before it starts by clearly informing all speakers ahead of time about your organization's policy regarding equal, unoffensive treatment. Give them details in the form of a formal meeting code or of a simple statement in the context of other information that they need to do an effective job with your audience. As an illustration, Control Data took the suggested meeting code presented later in this chapter and adapted it to its own situation:

At Control Data, affirmative action for women and minority-group members produced a typical pattern of results: First, these groups achieved greater representation in upper-level positions. Second, they participated in more meetings. Third, they complained about what they saw and heard at those meetings.

What is not typical (yet) is Control Data's response. Using the meeting code presented in this chapter, the company adopted its own, providing guidelines for meeting planners throughout the multinational operation of Control Data and its major subsidiary, Commercial Credit.

Such guidelines had been considered by Jaime Pedraza, Consultant for Affirmative Action for Women at Control Data, when she received a copy of Without Bias. *A note attached from David Noer, Commercial Credit Vice President, pointed out the meeting code. Control Data's own version quickly evolved.*

Other affirmative-action activities in the company smoothed the way for adoption of the code in late 1980. Presented as a set of guidelines, not as corporate policy, a printed booklet was distributed in early 1981. A cover memo to the 4,500 managers who received a copy summarized the information and underscored Control Data's equal-opportunity philosophy. The code is also included in the corporate manual of affirmative-action procedures.

Calls for more information and cooperation by company travel planners who help organize major meetings are early indications that the guidelines will be effective.

Subtle bias occurs in other instances of verbal communication in meetings. Congratulations, thanks, and other forms of recognition should be based on performance, not on irrelevant attributes. Like inappropriate introductions, these comments can belittle the efforts and success of participants, for example:

A woman in a middle-management job was unexpectedly called on to explain a new program to a committee of senior officers in her company. After an hour's presentation and having successfully fielded questions, she won approval of the program. Rising to thank her, the chairman surveyed the board room and offered, "I'm sure I speak for all of us. It was a pleasure to have such a pretty girl in our midst today."

Do not use terms such as "dear," "honey," or "girl," regardless of age or rank differences. Apply the same rules of courtesy to both male and female participants, for example, shaking hands. (Because some men may feel constrained by dated rules of etiquette, women might take the initiative here and in similar situations.)

Avoid behaving solicitously toward members of any group, especially people with disabilities. Encourage full participation and accept with respect and courtesy–and without condescension–the contributions of all those attending.

SUMMARY

1. Select meeting assistants based on ability, not on role stereotypes.
2. Select leaders and speakers who represent a cross-section of the organization.
3. Plan meeting facilities and schedules so that persons with disabilities can participate fully.
4. Depict people in meeting publicity in ways that are not stereotyping or demeaning.
5. Introduce speakers without alluding to sex, physical attributes, or other irrelevant qualities.
6. Design meeting entertainment and visuals so that they are not stereotyping or demeaning.
7. Consider the composition of the audience when preparing speeches and supporting materials.

ADDENDUM

A Meeting Code

To ensure that meetings are planned and conducted in an unbiased manner, an organization may want to develop a meeting code for distribution to those persons who plan, publicize, and conduct meetings. The code might also be given to outside speakers or consultants. Following is an example.

Preamble

The policy of this organization is to support equal opportunity for all, without discrimination because of race, color, religion, sex, national origin, disability, age, or sexual orientation.

This policy should be reflected in meetings that take place under the organization's auspices, including business, sales, or staff meetings, workshops or training sessions, conventions, conferences, annual meetings, or any other event sponsored by the organization.

We recognize that meetings are a form of communication that utilize a wide range of media, including interpersonal communication. They are, therefore, a powerful means to reinforce equal-opportunity commitment. Organization staff and consultants should be guided by this code when planning, publicizing, and conducting meetings.

One: Planning

Meeting Site and Schedule

Meeting facilities will be selected at sites where all may attend, regardless of race, color, religion, sex, national origin, disability, age, or sexual orientation.

We will select and arrange meeting facilities and time the schedule so that people with disabilities have complete access and can participate fully in all meeting activities.

Meeting Organization and Roles

Food and beverage planning, service, and clean-up; note-taking; meeting arrangements; hospitality and ushering duties, and similar assignments will be made according to ability, not role stereotypes.

Selection of Meeting Leaders

We will seek to select the best-qualified persons, while ensuring equal opportunity by exploring internal or external sources that include men and women from a range of ethnic or racial backgrounds and ages. Selection will be made without regard to race, color, religion, sex, national origin, disability, age, or sexual orientation.

When selecting a meeting chairperson, leader, moderator, or facilitator, especially from internal candidates, we will recognize the limits of always choosing from among higher ranks, which frequently do not include women and minority-group members. Where possible, we will seek to give developmental experience to these persons.

Two: Publicity

Fliers, posters, brochures, newspaper and magazine advertisements, radio and television spots, and other material used to promote a meeting will treat all groups with dignity and respect. Events will not be promoted by exploiting neither women nor men as sex objects or by using stereotypes of any group. We will seek to depict men and women of various ages, abilities, and racial and ethnic backgrounds in artwork and in casting for radio, television, and internal video material.

Three: Conducting the Meeting

Introductory Comments

We recognize that introductory comments set the tone of the meeting and affect how the person being introduced will be viewed and accepted. Therefore, we will frame introductions that are not condescending, stereotyping, or demeaning, but that foster equal acceptance and treatment of all groups.

Written Materials

When preparing written materials (such as handouts, commentaries, training worksheets, and scripts) for meetings, we will ensure effective communication by considering the audience. Unless otherwise the case, we will assume that audiences include both men and women of various ages, abilities, and racial and ethnic backgrounds. Meeting materials and language used by meeting leaders will reflect this mix. Material that is demeaning or stereotyping will be avoided.

Visual and Audiovisual Aids

We will make the same assumptions regarding audience as in written materials, unless otherwise the case. No group will be exploited or demeaned by the way it is depicted in visual or audiovisual aids.

Humor

We will refrain from humor (jokes and off-hand remarks) based on race, color, religion, sex, national origin, disability, age, or sexual orientation.

Entertainment

We will refrain from meeting entertainment that in either form or content is demeaning or stereotyping to any group.

Guest Activities

We will not assume that guests are invariably female. Whether planned for men or women, such activities will not be based on stereotyped assumptions of interests.

Four: Other Interpersonal Communication

Meeting Formalities

Shaking hands and other courtesies will be extended in the same way for all groups. Solicitous treatment of any meeting participant will be avoided.

Personal Comments

When giving recognition (or in any other context), we will avoid irrelevant references to female participants' appearance and charm, as well as similar personal comments about members of other groups.

Participation

We will encourage participation by members of all groups. Courteous, respectful listening will be emphasized, and condescension will be avoided.

PART 3

Translating Principles Into Policy

Chapter 8

Employee Communication Without Bias: A Continuing Program at Bank of America

Chapter 9

Equal Opportunity on Campus: Affirmative Action at Algonquin College

Chapter 10

Taking Bias Out of News: Progress in Public Media

Chapter 8

Employee Communication Without Bias: A Continuing Program at Bank of America

by Linda Cook Roberts

In 1981, Bank of America observed the seventh year of its affirmative-action program for employee communication. It began in 1974, as consciousness about bias in language was starting to develop. The program has spanned years during which public awareness and attitude changed greatly. Also, the bank's internal-communication function was extensively reorganized and expanded.

This case study summarizes development of the program and explores two questions:

- How does such an effort take hold and remain viable when the organization grows and the originators change functions or leave?

- What are today's challenges for nonbiased employee communication?

Developing the Program

The impetus to begin such a program may start with a critical incident or the attitude of the organization's communicators. At Bank of America, both factors were present.

The settlement by consent decree in 1974 of a class-action suit led internal communicators to examine their function with a critical eye. Were they reinforcing misconceptions and problems that surrounded equal-employment opportunity? Were they adequately reporting the facts about EEO policy and affirmative-action progress? More than that, should they take an active role in carrying out the spirit of the policy—in ways that would go beyond eliminating sexist and racist language and "girlie" photographs?

The answers to those current questions required a hard look at past performance at Bank of America. All issues of management and staff publications were surveyed. Evaluations were made on many counts:

- Were female employees pictured? If so, in what job functions? At what job levels?
- Were spokespersons for the bank and various bank units invariably white males?
- Was the same fact true of specialists selected as subject-matter experts for articles?
- Did female employees or employees of various ethnic heritages tend to appear only in social or human-interest features?

Weeks of research (which included a close reading of related laws) revealed that a legal umbrella covered the entire range of the communicator's audience, as detailed in Chapter 11. Therefore, the scope of the communication affirmative-action program would be no less broad. It would cover all employees—male, female, persons of all ethnic backgrounds, young and old, of all religions, and physical and mental abilities.

These specific objectives were set:

- To convey company commitment to the equal-employment-opportunity policy.
- To help develop a climate for acceptance and success of the affirmative-action plan and programs.
- To report progress in achieving affirmative-action goals.
- To encourage all employees to reach their highest career potentials.
- To depict a visual balance of females, persons of all ethnic heritages, and employees with disabilities, at all levels.
- To reflect in media the ethnic composition of the corporate staff.

In brainstorming sessions, the editorial group worked to translate these objectives into specific articles appropriate for the four employee and management publications. The titles were arranged into an editorial timetable for the year (see the accompanying sample) as a further way of ensuring achievement of affirmative-action goals.

Here, then, is the framework of Bank of America's affirmative-action program for communicators:

- Setting an over-all goal.
- Naming specific objectives.

- Defining strategies to ensure their achievement.
- Scheduling specific articles within an editorial plan for the year.

Editorial treatment was another aspect that needed thorough examination. During the months before and in recent brainstorming sessions, editors and writers had been formulating some "dos" and "don'ts." This process often happened on the run: "Let's do a story on a female manager of a branch office!" "Great . . . a role model. But, wait a minute . . . what's the *story*?"

Clearly, in this and similar suggestions, the story often was the sex or race of the person featured, leading to a solid "don't": the zoo approach that emphasizes the unusual. Typically "zooey" is the inevitable question, "How does it feel to be the first woman (disabled person, man) in this job?" Therefore, when such a story was suggested, the staff could joke, "Look, Ma! See the lady in her new job!" The idea would be modified or dropped.

A corollary "do" also was established: Make an extra effort to include a female, Asian, Black, or Spanish-surnamed employee, whenever appropriate, in a bona fide news story.

Implementing the Program and Tracking Results

For some communicators, a new attitude about nonbiased language or editorial approach wasn't easy to master. A process of grappling with new, even alien, ideas was necessary. Each person tossed out a few things, reserved opinion on others, and embraced some.

As this coming-to-terms proceeded, so did the editorial plans already scheduled. They provided a framework for progress toward the program's objectives and, in a sense, gave communicators room to kick around everyday decisions without getting bogged down or losing sight of the goal.

In addition, communication lines were established with staff members in the personnel and legal departments who had EEO responsibilities at Bank of America. Their cooperation proved invaluable.

After a year, results were evaluated. Improvements were seen in efforts to encourage career development. Some 40 stories had depicted female or minority-group employees as role models. The ethnic composition of the bank now was reflected in all staff publications because editors, writers, and photographers consciously had sought to include these groups in stories wherever their beats took them.

A new format that utilized a forum approach was particularly successful in broadening the range of employees appearing in *Management Magazine*. It featured a survey or interview of several key employees (or a panel discussion) to enable staff members who were subject-matter experts to appear in publications or on videotape.

Gradually, more subtle changes occurred. The use of the nongeneric "he" disappeared. Female, Black, Asian, and Spanish-surnamed employees made their way into photographs of the annual management conference, as they had made their way into higher management.

Ensuring a Continuing, Contemporary Program

Progress was tracked yearly thereafter, with counts of feature articles, photos, quotes, and other signs of the visibility of all employees in the organizational media, including print and video. This success continued to be measured, even though the bank's communication function experienced major reorganization, extensive promotion, and an increase of editorial personnel. In addition, the communication officer with responsibility for development and guidance of the program took on duties in another area and eventually left the bank.

These events are normal and inevitable ones that can influence the success of such a program. However, Bank of America points to three factors that account for its continued life and success.

First, the program was formal and management-supported in its development and implementation, rather than a campaign by one enlightened editor. Examples of this commitment are the presence from the start of department-head sanction and encouragement, the assignment of a person to develop the program, the writing and implementing of specific objectives, and regular measurement of results.

A second factor in the continuing success of the program was the editorial staff itself. Most of the women and men with editorial responsibilities had become or were already personally committed to bias-free communication. That point of view was informally, even unconsciously, communicated to others—new staff members, art directors, photographers, and so on. While no two writers or editors would agree on every question of wording or editorial approach, the basic nonbiased nature of all communication prevailed.

Finally, outside influences were favorable. Generally speaking, public media raised the issue (whether regarding television programming, advertising, educational publications, or other media), thus reinforcing the bank's internal program.

As a result of these three factors, the program has become less formal over time. It has become "mainstreamed" as part of the basic fabric of employee communication.

Equal, nonbiased treatment of all Bank of America employees has been achieved. The contemporary challenge of bias-free communication remains, ironically, that of continuing education (or, as it has been popularized, "consciousness-raising"). Bank communicators are very aware that internally, as in the general population, sensitivity to the issues is not achieved 100 percent of the time.

With the most basic aspects of nonbiased communication now finally in place, the need and opportunity exist to reinforce even the most fundamental messages. Of particular concern are those directed to persons in senior-level positions with 10 to 15 years remaining in their careers. They exert great influence over the attitudes toward, and career opportunities of, other employees.

These messages should be familiar. They include appropriate business behavior of male executives with female staff members at all levels, treatment of female professionals who are pregnant or who are mothers, portrayal of women in speeches and supporting materials, and awareness and reevaluation of the "old-boy" network that sometimes influences career success. Thus, the successes are won, but the torch passes, and the work continues.

SUMMARY

1. Study legal and company requirements for equal-employment-opportunity communication. Include laws, guidelines of the compliance agency for your industry, and your company's affirmative-action program.
2. Do a benchmark survey. Know what's been done in the past so progress can be measured and evaluated.
3. Adopt a policy regarding editorial treatment, language, art, and photography. Critique publications and work with staff to support that policy.
4. Write a list of objectives for equal-employment-opportunity communication. Involve company and communication-management personnel, as well as staff with legal and EEO responsibilities. Gain their support and assistance.
5. Plan ahead by drawing up editorial timetables. Specific story ideas and publication dates help achieve objectives.
6. Measure and evaluate progress. Renew and revise objectives and broaden the support and advisory bases for the program.

ADDENDUM

Editorial Timetable

A part of Bank of America's affirmative-action program for employee communication has been a timetable of articles and ideas for the coming months. Topics are suggested in cooperation with equal-opportunity and other personnel staff.

The material is tentatively scheduled by calendar quarter for each publication. Firm scheduling is subject to further research with sources. Editorial meetings take place regularly to assess progress and to continue the planning process.

Role Models

BankAmerican

1. *March* "Making of a Super Supervisor"—Example of effective female supervisor; women in visual composites of ideal supervisors.
2. *May* "How PIC Works"—Quotes female supervisors; describes career growth.
3. *May* "Foreign Exchange Trading Operations"—Depicts female officer now in training for one of four trading positions.
4. *May* New column on social policy—Photo and bylined material by female research officer.
5. *Fall* "Role of the Account Officer"—Will include female, minority-group officers, or both.
6. *Monthly* "On the Way Up"—Ongoing coverage of female/minority-group career advancement.

BankAmerican World

1. *January* "B of A's New Threshold to Europe" —European division featuring female personnel officer.
2. *April* "Foreign Exchange Trading Operations"—See *BankAmerican* No. 3.
3. *Quarterly* "Around the *BankAmerican World*"—News briefs regularly include female/minority-group employees in social activities.

Management Magazine

1. *April* Career development program follow-up—Forum of supervisors, including women/members of minority groups, give feedback on program.
2. Bona fide news article(s) to be bylined by female or minority-group officers (various times throughout the year).

Management Newsletter

Regular reporting of official promotions.

Education

BankAmerican

1. Mid-life person in business world.
2. From "Take a Letter" to "Ask the Computer"—Secretaries interviewed regarding job responsibilities.
3. *June–July* "How to Cope With Stress"—Men and women face executive pressures.

BankAmerican World

July "Preparing for a Transfer Abroad"—Includes female officer transferring to Caracas.

Management Magazine

1. Articles that dispel myths about female/minority-group workers.
2. New slants in management training—How training department helps supervisors incorporate new business ethics in managerial approach.
3. Reprint article by Dru Scott or other consultant on challenges faced by businesswomen.
4. Supervisor's role and responsibilities in area of equal opportunity.

Management Newsletter

Wall Street Journal story dispels myths regarding male/female turnover rates; Bank of America figures compared.

Career Development

BankAmerican

1. *May* "100 Top Jobs"—Role of management development committee; relate its goals to equal opportunity.
2. *August* New degree program of Consortium of California State Universities and Colleges.
3. *Fall* Employee guide to in-house training programs.
4. "How To Get the Most Out of Your Career Counseling Interview."
5. Decisive moments in BankAmerican's careers—Important promotions and how they happened.
6. Job-posting—Successes, progress, and future of the program.

Management Magazine

1. Training opportunities for managers.

2. Individual objective-setting and career-planning.
3. Supervisor's role and responsibilities in employee career development.
4. Bank officers relate experiences in management training programs given by university extensions; summary of community resources.

Management Newsletter

Career-development resources—Ideas from regional training officers.

Equal-Opportunity Policy, Goals, Timetables, Programs, Progress, Related Stories*

BankAmerican

1. Reorganization of equal-opportunity section—Interview restating policy, progress to date, goals, and so forth.
2. Production of film on equal opportunity and the individual employee—Storyboard approach to film's message.
3. Women's Trust and training—Success stories, tips on best utilization of available opportunities.

Management Magazine

Women assigned abroad—Who, when, how they are doing.

Management Newsletter

1. Suitable coverage acknowledging EEO compliance review.
2. Film on equal opportunity in production.

---

*Subject to guidance of equal-opportunity section.

Chapter 9

Equal Opportunity on Campus: Affirmative Action at Algonquin College

by Marianne Glofcheski Ménard

Women working and training at Algonquin College are in the classic double bind:

On the one hand, they need to get hired, help make decisions, be properly compensated, enjoy professional satisfaction, and stop being a minority.

On the other hand, they need to balance a career with what for many is a simultaneous responsibility—managing a home and family.

Through a commitment to equal opportunity and affirmative action, these needs of women have been translated into objectives for the college as *employer* and *teacher*. For the former, they are

- Adapting the selection process for jobs.

- Recognizing nontraditional, noninstitutional, work-related experience.
- Giving equal pay for work of equal value.
- Opening avenues for power and representation within the college.
- Offering career development in keeping with lifestyle.

The college as teacher has accepted a responsibility to women and men who need an environment where career choice is unrestrained by sex-role stereotypes.

Algonquin College is a community-based bilingual school of applied arts and technology. Fall 1981 full-time enrollment was some 9,000 and part-time 24,000, spread among 22 campuses and offices in a five-county area, which includes Canada's capital city of Ottawa. French and English are used in educational activities, and this bilingual requirement directly affects all administrative functions.

The Need for Affirmative Action

In late 1976, Algonquin appointed a special research team in response to a directive from the Ontario Ministry of Colleges and Universities, which required a status-of-women study at all colleges. Its accumulation of statistical and perceptual data revealed many problems faced by staff women at the school, among them the following:

- Some 40 percent of female employees got their jobs informally, skirting official selection procedures.

- Women were not in power, decision-making positions. No woman was a dean, and only 21 percent of important committee positions were occupied by women.
- A majority of women felt that their past job-related experience wasn't fairly credited in hiring or pay.
- Position and workload further isolated women in lower-paying jobs.
- The highest interest in professional development was shown by women; however, they were not encouraged to participate in such activities.

Specific findings related to communication were that

- Timely, bias-free information about resources and opportunities in the college was not readily available.
- The policy of bilingualism was frustrating. Unilingual anglophones felt that advancement was impossible, and bilingual francophones felt that having two languages meant doing two jobs.
- Departmental-based activities were seen as being most beneficial for communication among different personnel categories working together.

By May 1977, Algonquin administrators were able to adopt certain recommendations of the team. They included

- Creation of an Office of Equal Opportunities for three years.
- Revisions to selection boards, policies, and procedures to help assure unbiased consideration of women for jobs.

- Development of procedures to identify individual skills and encourage women to seek advancement in whatever way they define it.
- Expansion of existing orientation to include clarification about the job to be done, better integration of new employees into the department or office, and more information about the total college.
- A major analysis and revision of present job classifications and employee-assisted preparation of a job description for every position.
- Development of information and resources for career-oriented women and creation of frequent opportunities for women to meet.
- The requirement that all supervisors be responsible for development of their employees and that all employees have access to courses on performance evaluation.
- Promotion of professional-development activities aimed at an entire staff of a department or office.
- Open access by all part-time staff to college resources and establishment of universal salary scales for part-time teachers.

The college also adopted a policy on bilingualism, requiring second-language training for personnel in bilingual-designated administrative positions.

Program Response and Results

Under the direction of the Office of Equal Opportunities, these recommendations were addressed over the next three years. A major concern was a basic one: the need to inform both female and male staff and students of their opportunities at Algonquin. Equal opportunity "started at home" with our course offerings, then extended to the college as employer.

We began to find ways to recruit more female students into technical, trade, and business programs, as well as curricula in the more traditional areas of applied arts and health sciences. Women's programs were initiated in continuing education.

In health sciences, the problem was reversed in that we needed to interest more men in this area, previously considered a female-only curriculum.

To support these efforts (in addition to activities of the Office of Equal Opportunities related to female staff), an information bulletin was distributed regularly throughout the college. Action on all recommendations received other forms of communication assistance, as appropriate.

Through this program, Algonquin took a big step toward becoming an equal-opportunity institution, as measured by progress on all 1977 recommendations. Advances have seemed slow; however, results have depended on cooperation among two unions, the administrative-staff association, a senior committee of the college, the committee for equal opportunities, and the ministry. Communication has been an important element in bringing together these groups.

Many, many changes have occurred. In addition to progress in recruitment, selection, evaluation, and advancement of women at the college and changes in student-enrollment patterns, positive change has also been noted in the communication area:

- Information to staff about college resources is now available.
- We are abolishing sex-role stereotypes in materials related to offerings in health sciences, technology, and trades.
- Information and training workshops are available for staff and students, including continuing-education programs dealing with women at work.
- The equal-opportunities information bulletin is widely read with many appreciative comments.

Making Change Permanent

Equal opportunity has moved much closer to becoming institutionalized—an important step, because progress on 1977 objectives had to lead to long-term, permanent change.

To fulfill a mandate that equal-opportunity/affirmative-action objectives be part of a multiyear plan, Algonquin placed responsibility for them on managers since this group is accountable for over-all institutional objectives.

Communication support was, again, an integral part of the plan for 1980–81:

- Selection boards were to be thoroughly informed of sexist questions to be avoided.
- Information about career-development opportunities were to be readily available to all staff.
- A further effort was to be made to reduce sex-role stereotypes in literature on health careers. All materials distributed to the public were to be reviewed, alternative statements

and illustrations were to be developed for stereotypes found, and these suggestions were to be forwarded to literature sources.

- An "Algonquin Information Night for Women" was to be offered in the community each semester. Financial-assistance options available to full- and part-time students were to be emphasized and supported by a brochure.
- Career information and counseling sessions were to be conducted for students who are at Algonquin for retraining.
- An outreach program for secondary schools was to be developed to emphasize the wide range of career options for men and women and to reduce the influence of sex-role stereotypes.
- Secondary schools were to be encouraged to host "Career Awareness for Women" sessions, which would stress some of the pitfalls of not considering long-term career choices. Support materials would include a brochure on nontraditional career options and a film on technical careers.
- A series of information sheets was to present changing roles of women and career choices for young women.
- A half-day session was to sensitize placement officers, counselors, and admissions staff to the importance of career goals for young women and the financial implications of their choices.

These activities are illustrative of the role that communication has played in equal-opportunity progress at Algonquin. With creative programs and sensitized administrators to back up bias-free information, we hope to influence the other side of the bind for working women: incorporating career goals into home and family responsibilities.

SUMMARY

1. A commitment to equal opportunity on campus encompasses the school as both employer and teacher.
2. Promotional materials must be bias-free in words and visuals to reinforce equal entry into training programs.
3. Young women need comprehensive information early in the career-planning process to emphasize options and combat sex-role stereotypes.
4. Effective communication at the departmental level is a primary ingredient in improving the work environment and expanding advancement opportunities of employees.
5. A requirement for bilingual skills should be supported by access to language training.

Chapter 10

Taking Bias Out of News: Progress in Public Media

by Clara Degen and Judy E. Pickens, ABC[1]

"Words are no deeds," wrote Shakespeare in *Henry VIII*. This wisdom is especially true of the principles of bias-free communication presented earlier in this book. They do no good until they become deeds.

Most people are exposed to these deeds in public, rather than organizational, media. Newspapers, magazines, radio, and television touch everyone to some degree and, thus, have a great opportunity to reinforce or dispel bias. Yet

[1]The authors acknowledge the contributions to this chapter of the media mentioned, which are only selected examples of current media practice.

perhaps because they have become so diverse, complex, and powerful, they have been slower than the more easily governed corporate or association media to develop and act on sensitivity to bias.

That sensitivity is, however, evolving, and this chapter presents a sampling of progress. Awareness of racism led to awareness of sexism in public media, as it did in society at large. A few years ago, many media drafted statements and adopted them as policy in these two areas, whereas other sensitivities (such as to disability or age) have not yet been given comparable attention. They are, in general, riding on the coattails of earlier policy, rather than having their own place in style manuals.

The responsibility of public media to report and document without bias is historic, although only in recent years have theories about social responsibility been interpreted to include women and members of minority and other "protected" groups. For example, "Why Women Cannot Vote" was published by a learned journal in 1904, juxtaposed elsewhere in its pages by these words of Joseph Pulitzer: "Without high ethical ideals a newspaper not only is stripped of its splendid possibilities of public service, but may become a positive danger to the community."[2]

His "ethical ideals" began to have relevance by 1922 when they were supported by the Canons of Journalism adopted by the American Society of Newspaper Editors. Now known as "A Statement of Principles," these ideals (as revised) include the following statements:

---

[2]Joseph Pulitzer, "The College of Journalism," *The North American Review*, CLXXVIII (May, 1904), 667.

> *Good faith with the reader is the foundation of good journalism. Every effort will be made to assure that the news content is accurate, free from bias and in context, and that all sides are presented fairly.*
>
> *Journalists should respect the rights of people involved in the news, observe the common standards of decency and stand accountable to the public for the fairness and accuracy of their news reports.*[3]

While these principles speak more to partisan bias and fairness than to treatment of any group of people, they do open the door to positive interpretation, such as occurred in 1947. The report that year of the U.S. Commission on Freedom of the Press laid a broad foundation for media responsibility as we know it today in the United States.[4] This group of private citizens listed five requirements of public media, in both concept and performance:

1. Media should report the truth in context, separating fact from opinion.
2. Media should provide a forum for exchange of comment and criticism so that various views are known.
3. Media should present a representative picture of all segments of society, accurately portraying groups and discouraging stereotypes.

---

[3]American Society of Newspaper Editors, "A Statement of Principles" (1922, revised 1975).

[4]Commission on Freedom of the Press, *A Free and Responsible Press* (Chicago: University of Chicago Press, 1947).

4. Media should assume a responsibility to educate by reporting realistically.
5. Media should disseminate news as widely as possible so that all citizens can make informed decisions.

The third requirement established the framework for specific actions on equal treatment adopted and practiced by some media today.

Wire Services

In the United States, a strong influence on what the public receives is exerted by the two major wire services: Associated Press (AP) and United Press International (UPI). For more than 20 years, AP and UPI have set writing and editing style for newspapers, radio, and (to a lesser extent) magazines and television. Many media have their own stylebooks tailored to local situations; however, AP and UPI style is usually at their core. The influence of these guides (which are substantially the same) is further ingrained in our public media by their extensive use in journalism schools.

In 1977, a joint committee expanded and revised AP and UPI style in recognition of social changes; each year since, the services have considered additional revisions.[5,6] Reflected in these new guidelines and the individual versions that they have spawned are concerns about equal treatment of various groups, especially the sexes.

[5]Howard Angione, ed., *Associated Press Stylebook and Libel Manual* (New York: Associated Press, 1980).

[6]Bobby Ray Miller, ed., *The UPI Stylebook: A Handbook for Writers and Editors* (New York: United Press International, 1977).

Sex

While AP and UPI assert that women should receive the same treatment as men in all areas of coverage, action doesn't necessarily follow.

Wire-service practice is not to use courtesy titles for men but to use them for women. "Mrs." is used in first and second references if the woman uses her husband's first name ("Mrs. Samuel Foster," "Mrs. Foster"). A married woman who uses her own first name still has the title of "Mrs." in second reference, unless she expressly requests "Ms." ("Irene Foster," "Mrs. Foster"). A married, divorced, or widowed woman who uses her own full name is labeled as "Miss" by AP, unless she prefers "Ms."

A single woman gets a "Miss" or "Ms." in second reference. If she is divorced or widowed and still uses her husband's last name, she is "Mrs." in second reference, unless she objects.

This complex guideline on courtesy titles was opposed by Women in Communications, Inc., as not yet parallel with the policy of no marital designation for men. UPI allows such neutrality only when a woman prefers "Ms." and marital status is not relevant to the story.

In line with recommendations in Chapter 2 of this book, wire-service reporters and editors are not to use physical descriptions, sexist references, demeaning stereotypes, and condescending phrases in regard to either sex. Also banned are the assumption of male-only when both sexes are involved, surprise at women's accomplishments, and inclusion of family relationship when not relevant. "Lady" and "gentleman" are limited by AP and UPI to specific reference to fine manners.

The wire services counsel against coined words

("chairperson," "spokesperson"), except when directly quoted or when used in official descriptions. Alternatives are neutral titles ("leader," "representative") or specific ones designating the appropriate sex ("chairman," "spokeswoman").

Either "man" or "mankind" is acceptable to AP and UPI when both sexes are involved and when no other term is convenient. They suggest, however, looking at alternatives such as "humanity," "person," or "individual."

A nickname for either sex is used by itself only if the person prefers ("Jimmy Carter"). Otherwise, AP and UPI clearly indicate that it is a nickname ("Katherine 'Kitten' Turner").

Race

Wire-service style now addresses the use of dialects—and indicates that they are to be avoided (even in direct quotations), unless clearly relevant to the story. Vocabulary and pronunciation typical of a region or group can be interpreted as substandard or illiterate, they advise. Similarly, UPI avoids colloquialisms (such as "ain't") that the dictionary identifies as substandard.

AP and UPI style specifically prohibits words such as "wampum," "brave," and "squaw" because they can be disparaging of and offensive to Native North Americans.

Proper names of nationalities, peoples, races, and tribes ("Negro," "Sioux") are uppercase, while common names ("black," "white") are lowercase. Derogatory terms ("honky," "nigger") are lowercase and closely restricted to direct quotations essential to a story.

"Rightist," "leftist," and similar words are not

precise descriptions of political philosophies and, thus, are not used by either AP or UPI.

Age

"Elderly" and "senior citizen" are used by the wire services only for people 65 or older, but not in casual reference and never to refer to a specific person. If a deterioration of faculties is to be shown, exact words are used ("loss of hearing," "limited by arthritis").

Wire services follow local practice in reporting the name of someone under 18 convicted of a crime, unless a compelling reason exists to the contrary (such as a 16-year-old tried and convicted of a felony as an adult).

Newspapers

These current wire-service guidelines apply to their reporters and editors, but as was mentioned earlier, individual media frequently tailor and expand them to fit local situations. *The Los Angeles Times* and *The New York Times* are two highly influential examples. Each has an extensive style manual for its own pages and syndicated material.[7, 8] Both have many similarities with AP and UPI, but some notable differences.

---

[7]Frederick Holley, ed., *The Los Angeles Times Stylebook* (New York: The New American Library, Inc., 1981).

[8]Lewis Jordan, ed., *The New York Times Manual of Style and Usage* (New York: The New York Times Book Co., 1976).

Sex

The following listing summarizes their varying treatment of men and women:

THE LOS ANGELES TIMES	THE NEW YORK TIMES
For men, use first name, middle initial (if used), and last name in first reference and last name only thereafter.	Use first name, middle initial (if used), and last name in first reference and "Mr." thereafter. It is dropped when referring to preeminent men no longer living ("Lincoln," "Churchill") and not used in the sports section.
For women, use the same style as for men: last name only in second reference. Historic or prominent women may have courtesy titles ("Mme. Curie," "Mrs. Onassis").	Use a woman's first name in first reference and "Mrs." or "Miss" (as appropriate) thereafter. It is dropped when referring to preeminent women no longer living ("Bernhardt," "Woolf").
Courtesy titles are acceptable in quotations, "society" material, obituaries, and in instances of serious accident when using just a last name might appear callous.	Use "Ms." only in quoted material. Use "Miss" in second reference to a woman who is or has been married but who is not known by her married name ("Marian Anderson," "Miss Anderson"). Include a woman's orginal family name with her husband's, if she prefers this style ("Margaret Chase Smith").

Don't use a husband's name when a married woman is in the news because of her own activities, including in an obituary. However, if the woman is better known for her husband's activities, use his name in the obituary and headline ("Stella Peters, wife of William A. Peters"; "Mrs. William A. Peters Dies").

First names can be used in subsequent reference if two or more subjects have the same last name. Make the relationship clear ("Bob Spring and his brother, Ira;" "Louise Jordan and her husband, Stan").

Explaining a woman's choice of name (". . . as she prefers to be known") is patronizing and clouds clear writing. Communicate a relevant relationship otherwise ("Theresa Scott, wife of Larry Olmstead").[9]

"Representative" or "member of Congress" is preferred by both newspapers, instead of "congressman" or "congresswoman" (which can be used in specific reference). *The New York Times,* however, considers "chairman" generic.

The Los Angeles Times counsels caution in using substitutes for such words as "mankind" or "man-made" because meaning can be distorted. Similarly, alternatives to "actress" and "waitress"

[9]*The New York Times,* "Winners & Sinners," No. 403 (January 9, 1981).

may be awkward. *New York Times* readers may see "boyfriend" or "girlfriend" but only when a more tasteful and precise substitute can't be found when referring to adults. "Better half" and "bride" when "spouse" or "wife" is meant are recognized as offenses to be avoided. More precise characterizations are used for "housewife," whenever possible, because of the disparaging meaning that word has come to have.

Both newspapers choose "homosexual" over "gay," unless used in a formal title or quoted matter.

Race

The Los Angeles Times has added the following practices to AP and UPI style in the area of race:

- "Latino" is used to encompass all Spanish-surnamed groups in the United States.
- "Illegal aliens" is preferred to "illegal immigrants," "illegal migrants," "undocumented workers," or "undocumented aliens." None of these terms is accurate unless a person has been officially designated as such by the government. "Wetback" should be restricted to direct quotations.
- "Asian" or "Asian-American" is preferred to "Oriental."

The New York Times uses dialect, although it asks reporters not to try to duplicate spelling but rather to let choice of words and oddity of sentence construction convey dialect. Other style decisions related to race:

- *Times* editors campaign against the use of "minorities" ("women and minorities") when "members of minorities" or "members of minority groups" is intended.[10]

- "Ethnic" as a noun is similarly condescending; "ethnic groups," "ethnic background," or reference to a specific group ("Poles," "Germans") is preferred.[11]
- Relevance of racial, religious, or other heritage must be not only clear to the reporter but also demonstrated in copy so that readers aren't left to assume. An interesting, but unconnected, fact can be offensive ("Born of Italian parents, they established a steel-fabricating company." ". . . they established a successful chain of Italian restaurants.").[12]
- "Chicano" is used in references to United States citizens or residents of Mexican descent.
- "Chinaman" is disparaging and not used, unless in direct quotations.

Age

The *Los Angeles Times* uses only a child's first name in second reference. However, *The New York Times* uses "Mr." or "Miss" for a young person, unless a first name is less awkward. It also repeats the full name, rather than use "young" ("Young Kato," "Kim Kato").[13] The latter newspaper approves of "teen-age" as an adjective but avoids "teen," unless referring to a span of years. Reporters are asked to mention adoption only when clearly pertinent because of the word's

[10]Ibid., No.404 (March 13, 1981).
[11]Ibid., No.401 (November 7, 1980).
[12]Ibid., No. 400 (September 5, 1980).
[13]Ibid., No. 398 (December 14, 1979).

implication of second-class status that can be harmful to the children involved.[14]

On the other side of the age spectrum, *The New York Times* especially avoids "grandmother," unless relevant (and accurate) and unless "grandfather" would be used if the subject were a man.

Veteran Status

Because of the current stigma that such usage can reinforce, *The New York Times* avoids mention of Vietnam-veteran status when labeling someone accused of a crime, unless clearly pertinent ("The Vietnam veteran had a long arrest record." "The judge was lenient because of testimony supporting the influence on the defendant of three years as a P.O.W. in Vietnam.").[15]

Radio and Television

Broadcast journalism, with its different techniques, regulations, and rapid expansion, has interpreted ethics in some areas differently from print media, although they share similar principles.

The Code of Broadcast News Ethics of the Radio and Television News Directors Association states, "Broadcast news presentations shall be designed not only to offer timely and accurate information, but also to present it in the light of relevant circumstances that give it meaning and perspective."[16] This standard is interpreted to

---

[14]Ibid., No. 404 (March 13, 1981).
[15]Ibid., No. 403 (January 9, 1981).
[16]Radio and Television News Directors Association, "Code of Broadcast News Ethics" (1949).

mean that race, creed, nationality, prior status, and other such factors will be reported only when relevant. It is limited to news, only one side of broadcasting. Radio and television also entertain and, if commercial, include selling as an objective.

A look at current broadcast programming (whether public-supported or commercial) reveals a difference between news and entertainment in their approach to bias in communication. In general, greater attention is placed on this concern in news because its intent is to report facts, not be humorous or dramatic. Therefore, guidelines regarding bias are more often found on the news side. An example is the extensive set of production standards adopted by CBS News for all network activities.

Although it has not detailed "dos" and "don'ts" as have the print media mentioned earlier, CBS News has addressed bias in a statement on broadcast of objectionable material. It counsels CBS News personnel to consider carefully contemporary community standards, and general standards of news judgment and responsibility, before deciding on broadcasting material that might offend substantial portions of the audience. The policy advises including objectionable language only if warranted by the nature of a news event and the importance of reporting it. The degree of potential objection should also be considered. A similar policy can be detected behind announcements by radio and television stations, warning that material to follow might be objectionable to some members of the audience.

Categories of offensive material are not mentioned in the CBS News policy. However, the general wording leaves room for broad interpretation to include racial slurs, sexist references, and other bias.

SUMMARY

1. Public media have long-established precedent for bias-free communication but only recently have exhibited substantial application to groups protected by equal-opportunity laws.
2. Media policy is more clear in regard to sex and race; detailed practices regarding other areas of potential bias have not yet evolved.
3. Although media vary in choice of style, they are showing a growing sensitivity to the influence of language, especially the print media.

PART 4

Resources and References

Chapter 11

Equal-Employment-Opportunity Laws: Some Words to the Wise

Chapter 12

For Further Information

Chapter 11

Equal-Employment-Opportunity Laws: Some Words to the Wise

by Catherine M. Meek[1]

In the beginning was the Word: Thou shalt not discriminate. Then came the Sentence: Thou shalt not discriminate and thou shalt take affirmative action. Now we have the Paragraph.

In the United States, the proliferation of equal-employment laws, regulations, and guidelines since the early sixties has been dramatic.[2] In 1964, Title VII of the Civil Rights Act

[1]Susan Nichols, Public Information Director for the American Cancer Society, Los Angeles Coastal Cities Unit, contributed this chapter in the first edition.

[2]This information outlines laws related to equal-employment opportunity that were current at the time of publication. The criteria governing applications of some U.S. laws may now be somewhat different. It is presented as a summary, not as legal advice.

provided the foundation. Now, the list (depending on specific state and municipal laws) includes

- Race
- Color
- Religion
- Sex
- National origin
- Disability
- Age
- Marital status
- Sexual orientation
- Veteran status
- Pregnancy
- Medical condition
- Arrest or conviction record

In Canada, human-rights legislation may include prohibition against discrimination on the basis of

- Race
- Color
- Religion
- Sex
- National or ethnic origin
- Disability
- Age
- Marital status
- Sexual orientation
- Language orientation
- Family status
- Political belief

Legal requirements for equal-employment opportunity and affirmative-action are continually evolving and increasingly complex. They are also becoming an integral part of doing business in North America. Thus, the communicator has an important obligation and opportunity: to help organizations make the law understandable and to support an equal-opportunity climate in organizations and communities.

Laws in the United States

Numerous laws currently exist prohibiting various forms of job discrimination:

Title VII of the Civil Rights Act of 1964 prohibits discrimination because of race, color, religion, sex, or national origin in all employment practices. The Equal Employment Opportunity Commission (which administers Title VII) has issued guidelines on discrimination because of sex, religion, national origin, and employee-selection procedures. These guidelines may be found in Title 29 of the Code of Federal Regulations, Parts 1604–1607.

Executive Order No. 11246 (1965) prohibits federal contractors and subcontractors from discriminating on the basis of race, color, religion, sex, or national origin. As amended by *Executive Order No. 11375*, this order covers employers with federal contracts or subcontracts in excess of $10,000 and financial institutions holding federal funds or which are agents for United States bonds and notes.

Revised Executive Order No. 4 requires affected employers to develop a written affirmative-action program to correct any under-utilization of women and members of minority groups. This order applies to all nonconstruction contractors and subcontractors with federal contracts in excess of $50,000 and 50 or more employees.

The Equal Pay Act of 1963 prohibits

discrimination on the basis of sex in salaries and fringe benefits.

The Age Discrimination in Employment Act of 1967, as amended, prohibits discrimination against persons aged 40 to 70 in all terms, conditions, and privileges of employment.

The Vocational Rehabilitation Act of 1973 requires affirmative steps to recruit, hire, and promote qualified persons who have (or are regarded as having) disabilities. Section 503 applies to federal contracts or subcontracts in excess of $2,500; Section 504 applies to institutions that receive federal financial assistance.

The Vietnam Era Veterans Readjustment Assistance Act of 1974 requires similar steps in regard to disabled veterans. Section 402 covers employers with federal contracts or subcontracts in excess of $10,000.

Most states and many local governments prohibit discrimination on the same grounds as federal laws. However, many states have added other bases. These laws apply when they are more stringent than federal minimum standards that protect employee rights.

Laws in Canada

All jurisdictions in Canada have some form of legislation to ensure the right of equal opportunity in employment. The grounds upon which discrimination is prohibited are basically the same in federal and provincial jurisdictions: race, color, religion, sex, and national or ethnic origin.

Other grounds have been added in certain areas. The federal jurisdiction that is covered by the Canadian Human Rights Act includes age, marital status, conviction for which a pardon has been granted, and physical disability. Many of the ten provinces and two territories have added similar bases. For example, political belief or opinion is a proscribed ground in Quebec, British Columbia, and Newfoundland and on Prince Edward Island.

Guidelines interpreting these various statutes have been issued and cover job advertisements, employment applications, interviews, equal pay, and employee benefits.

In Canada, affirmative action is voluntary. Human-rights legislation in most jurisdictions allows for the development of "special programs" for protected employees. It permits and promotes affirmative action but does not require it.

Communicators with an audience in Quebec should be aware that National Assembly of Quebec Bill 101 dictates French as the official language. See Chapter 1 for more information on its requirements.

How Legislation Affects Communication

Affirmative-action programs in the United States must contain a policy statement outlining an organization's commitment to affirmative action. In addition, this policy must be communicated to employees within the organization and to external sources, such as employment agencies, suppliers, and community groups. Such communications include employee manuals, company publications, training programs, annual reports, and advertisements.

As part of their regular compliance review, federal contract-compliance officers may inspect these materials and other media to see if the company is complying with the regulations and if women, minority-group members, and other protected groups are presented in a nondiscriminatory light. Furthermore, employees and community agencies may be interviewed by compliance officers to see if they understand the company's policy and if that policy is being distributed.

In Canada, employment advertisements that imply either directly or indirectly that any prohibited ground of discrimination may be a preference for employment are considered illegal. In addition, the use of nondiscriminatory job titles is required. This mandate may cause the use of a neutral job title ("salesperson"), dual titles ("salesman/woman"), or a phrase explaining that the position is open to both sexes. Antidiscrimination laws may also apply to pictures and nonverbal advertisements where a preference (and, therefore, a limitation on applications) is implied—for example, a picture of a male for a management position.

Testing the Media

Ask a few questions when reviewing your media, whether they be feature articles, video programs, news releases, or interoffice memoranda. How might sensitized women, members of minority groups, or persons with disabilities interpret a given medium from their points of view? Would it be acceptable? Would an article about a woman have been written the same way if the subject had been a man?

Look beyond titles or names to a medium's tone

and underlying concept. When testing an entire publication, look at the over-all product. Taken as a whole, are women and minority-group members adequately represented in both graphics and writing? Are older people or those with disabilities stereotyped in their representation?

Does your company's annual report include information about affirmative action? According to a random survey of 1979 annual reports, only 25 percent of the Fortune 1,000 industrial firms and top financial institutions made specific reference to affirmative action or equal-employment opportunity.[3]

A balance should be struck in a medium, considered in its entirety. Other chapters in this book should prove helpful to the communicator on this point.

When featuring employees in articles or other media that describe your company's affirmative-action programs (including those about race, sex, or disability), remember that the subjects' right to privacy must be considered. Make certain that persons featured or pictured in these portrayals are aware of how the information will be used. You may want to secure releases.

Recently issued guidelines in the United States on sexual harassment and national origin point to the need for clearly defined policies and procedures to be communicated to all supervisors and employees.[4] For example, the compliance agency suggests that employers express disapproval of sexual harassment by publishing

[3]Survey conducted by Barnhill Hayes, Inc., Milwaukee, WI.
[4]These guidelines have been issued by the Equal Employment Opportunities Commission as part of its Title VII authority.

policies prohibiting such harassment by any employee.

The Communicator's Role

Communicators who conform their efforts to equal-employment and affirmative-action legislation and policies are doing their employers a large favor. Keeping media in compliance with the law is, for starters, good business. A company or medium that offends significant segments of the population can find itself the target of negative publicity and consumer boycotts. Nonadherence to laws and policies also can have long-range, bread-and-butter ramifications: Media that are in compliance with laws and policies are sensible insurance in the event claims are filed against the company.

The communicator need not be defensive about an organization's affirmative-action record. Report significant strides toward achieving affirmative-action goals and timetables. The approach should be one of showing the employer as being responsive to the times and to requirements of new and unprecedented legislation.

Equal employment and affirmative action are no longer matters of good faith on anyone's part. Legislation currently exists in most of North America covering almost every condition of employment. The effective communicator will recognize and reflect this fact in all aspects of organizational communication.

Discrimination under the law has a very specific meaning that does not come through sensitivity; it must be learned. Make a habit of seeking the advice of legal and affirmative-action staff members. Their special expertise and familiarity with new and changing laws could help keep the communicator—and the organization—from violating legal requirements.

SUMMARY

1. Legislation currently covers almost all aspects of equal-employment opportunity in North America, and the prudent communicator should reflect this fact in all media.
2. Any company that is reviewed for compliance with equal-employment and affirmative-action directives in the United States may have its media examined, and employees and community agencies may be questioned about their knowledge of the company's employment-opportunity policy.
3. An organization's media should withstand testing from the perspective of sensitized women, members of minority groups, or other persons whose employment rights are guaranteed by the law.

Chapter 12

For Further Information

by Myra L. Kruger

The following references may assist in understanding in greater detail and in practicing bias-free communication. This list is not meant to be definitive but rather is a compilation of materials known to and used by contributors to this book.

Where possible, entries are annotated to help explain their purpose or content. Also, addresses are given for most groups and publications.

Affirmative-Action Laws and Their Implementation

United States

Anderson, Howard J., ed. *Primer of Equal Employment Opportunity* (1978). Bureau of National Affairs, 1231 25th St., N.W., Washington, DC 20037.

Chrysalis Center. Guidelines, corporate case histories, and background on sexual harassment. 2104 Stevens Ave., Minneapolis, MN 55404.

Council on Interracial Books for Children. Compilation of all work to date and free catalog available on bias-free materials, including sexism, racism, ageism, and disability, as well as consulting services in awareness training. 1841 Broadway, New York, NY 10023.

Human-rights offices in all states.

International Association of Business Communicators, Affirmative Action Committee. 870 Market St., Suite 940, San Francisco, CA 94102.

President's Committee on Employment of the Handicapped. *Handbook of Legal Rights of Handicapped People* (1976). 1111 20th St., N.W., Washington, DC 20036.

Racism and Sexism Resource Center for Educators. Reprints, curricula files, bibliographies, studies, and training programs. 1841 Broadway, New York, NY 10023.

U.S. Department of Labor, Employment Standards Administration. *Age Discrimination in Employment Act of 1967*, WH Publication 1387. 200 Constitution Ave., N.W., Washington, DC 20210.

U.S. Department of Labor, Equal Employment Opportunity Commission. Branch offices in all states. 2401 E St., N.W., Washington, DC 20506. *National Origin Guidelines.* Address above.

U.S. Federal Register, volumes January 19, 1979; March 2, 1979; April 20, 1979; February 1, 1980; April 11, 1980; September 19, 1980; October 21, 1980. 1100 L St., N.W., Washington, DC 20005.

Canada

Affirmative Action Resource Centre, Canadian Employment and Immigration Commission. 2 Place du Portage, Hull, Quebec K1A 0J2.

Canadian Advisory Council on the Status of Women. Similar offices in provinces. 151 Sparks St., P.O. Box 1541, Station B, Ottawa, Ontario K1P 5R5.

Canadian Human Rights Commission. Branch offices in most major cities. Jackson Building, 257 Slater St., Ottawa, Ontario K1A 1E1.

Canadian Union of Public Employees. *Equal Opportunity at Work: A CUPE Affirmative Action Manual* (1976). 21 Florence St., Ottawa, Ontario K1P 0W6.

Centre/Bureau De La Main D'oevre Feminine. *Affirmative Action Guidelines for Employers* (undated). Information Centre Officer, 2 Place du Portage, Hull, Quebec K1A 0J2.

Department of Indian and Northern Affairs, Policy Coordination. 10 Wellington St., Hull, Quebec K1A 0H4.

Developmental Personnel, Policies and Activities Division, Personnel Policy Branch of the Treasury Board of Canada. Place Bell, Ottawa, Ontario K1A 0R5.

Office of the Coordinator of Affirmative Action, Ontario Ministry of Colleges and Universities.

Mowat Block, Queen's Park, Toronto, Ontario M7A 1L2.

Office of Equal Opportunities for Women, Public Service Commission. L'Esplanade Laurier, West Tower, 300 Laurier Ave. W., B-1559, Ottawa, Ontario K1A 0M7.

Women's Bureau, Rights in Employment Branch of Labour Canada. Other Women's Bureau offices in provinces, under auspices of labour ministries. 400 University Ave., Toronto, Ontario M7A 1T7.

Europe

Institute of Personnel Management. 5 Wimsley St., Oxford Circus, London, England W1N 2AQ.

International Labour Office. *Equality of Opportunity and Treatment for Women Workers*, Report VIII of the International Labour Conference (1975). 4 Route Des Morillons, CH-1211 Genève 22, Switzerland.

General References

Angione, Howard, ed. *Associated Press Stylebook and Libel Manual* (1980). Associated Press, 50 Rockefeller Plaza, New York, NY (U.S.) 10020.

Bank of America. *Guidelines for the Equal Treatment of All Employees in Bank of America Internal Communication* (1975). Communications Department #3631, P.O. Box 37000, San Francisco, CA (U.S.) 94137.

Committee on Social Issues. *Statement on Bias-Free Materials* (1976). Association of American Publishers, One Park Ave., New York, NY (U.S.) 10016.

Conseil E'conomique du Canada. *Des Travailleurs et des Emplois: Une Étude du Marche du*

Travail au Canada (1976). Information Canada, 2 Place du Portage, Hull, Quebec (Canada) K1A 0J2.

Control Data. *Guidelines for Eliminating Bias From Meetings* (1980). Booklet of procedures for corporate meeting planners. Office of the Consultant, Affirmative Action for Women, P.O. Box O, Minneapolis, MN (U.S.) 55440.

Cruz, Daisy. "Affirmative Action at Work." *Personnel Journal* (U.S.) LV, No. 5 (1976), 226–27, 250.

Cunningham, John. "Avoiding Common Pitfalls in Affirmative Action Programs." *Personnel Journal* (U.S.), LV, No. 3 (1976), 124–27, 136.

Farmer, Marilyn, and Peter Smith. "A Practical Approach to Equal Opportunity." *Personnel Management* (U.S.), IX, No. 3 (1977), 10–20.

Gery, Gloria. "Hiring Minorities and Women: The Selection Process." *Personnel Journal* (U.S.), LIII (December, 1974), 906–909.

Goffman, Erving. "Genderisms: Reinforcement of Stereotypes in Advertising." *Psychology Today* (U.S.), XI (August, 1977), pp. 60–63.

Holley, Frederick, ed. *The Los Angeles Times Stylebook* (1981). The New American Library, Inc., 1633 Broadway, New York, NY (U.S.) 10019.

International Association of Business Communicators. "Speaker Policies." Brochure for IABC speakers, which includes a statement about bias-free meetings. 870 Market St., Suite 940, San Francisco, CA (U.S.) 94102.

Jordan, Lewis, ed. *The New York Times Manual of Style and Usage* (1976). The New York Times Book Company, 10 E. 53rd St., New York, NY (U.S.) 10022.

MacMillan Publishing Company. *Guidelines for Creating Positive Sexual and Racial Images in*

Educational Materials (1975). School Division Committee, 866 Third Ave., New York, NY (U.S.) 10022.

Mathers, Catherine J., and Marnie Shea. *Affirmative Action: A Selected Bibliography* (1975). Ontario Ministry of Labour, Research Branch, 400 University Ave., Toronto, Ontario (Canada) M7A 1T7.

Mepham, George J. *Equal Opportunity and Equal Pay: A Review of Objectives, Problems and Progress* (1974). Institute of Personnel Management, 5 Wimsley St., Oxford Circus, London (England) W1N 7AQ.

Miller, Bobby Ray, ed. *The UPI Stylebook: A Handbook for Writers and Editors* (1977). United Press International, 220 E. 42nd St., New York, NY (U.S.) 10017.

Moore, Joy, and Frank Laverty. "Affirmative Action: A Sadly Passive Event." *The Business Quarterly* (Canada), XL, No. 4 (1975), 22–29.

Pié, Bette. "Affirmative Action: Can the Voluntary Approach Work?" *The Business Quarterly* (Canada), XLI, No. 1 (1976), 15–19.

"Stepped Up Drive Against Job Discrimination." *Association Management* (U.S.) XXVI, No. 5, (1974), 55–58.

Worth, Sol. *Studies in Anthropology of Visual Communication*, Society for the Anthropology of Visual Communication, 3620 Walnut St., Philadelphia, PA (U.S.) 19104.

Race

Council on Interracial Books for Children. *Guidelines for Selecting Bias-Free Textbooks and Storybooks* (1980). Racism and Sexism

Resource Center for Educators, 1841 Broadway, New York, NY (U.S.) 10023.
Daniel, Jack L. "The Facilitation of White-Black Communication." *The Journal of Communication* (U.S.), XX (June, 1970), 134–41.
McGraw-Hill Book Company. *Multi-Ethnic Guidelines* (1973). Webster/McGraw-Hill Division, Editing and Styling, 1221 Avenue of the Americas, New York, NY (U.S.) 10020.
Moore, Robert B., ed. *Racism in the English Language* (1976). Racism and Sexism Resource Center for Educators, 1841 Broadway, New York, NY (U.S.) 10023.
Rich, Andrea L. "Some Problems in Interracial Communications: An Interracial Group Case Study." *Central States Speech Journal* (U.S.), XXII, No. 4 (1971), 228–35.

Sex

American Press Women. "Guidelines to Eliminate Sexism in the Media." *Press Women* (U.S.), XXXIX (January, 1976), 6.
Bennett, James E. "Equal Opportunities for Women: Why and How Companies Should Take Action." *The Business Quarterly* (Canada), XL, No. 4 (1975), 22–29.
Bennett, James E., and Pierre M. Loewe. *Women in Business: A Shocking Waste of Human Resources* (1975). MacLean-Hunter, Ltd., 481 University Ave., Toronto, Ontario (Canada) M5W 1A7.
Benson, Rosen, and Thomas H. Jerdee. "Sex Stereotyping in the Executive Suite." *Harvard Business Review* (U.S.), LII, No. 2 (1974), 45–58.

Centre for Continuing Education. *Report: Western Conference on Opportunities for Women* (1973). University of British Columbia and Vancouver, 6328 Memorial Rd., Vancouver, British Columbia (Canada) V6T 1W5.

Crull, Peggy. *Impact of Sexual Harassment on the Job: A Profile of the Experiences of 92 Women*, Research Report No. 3 (1979). Working Women's Institute, 593 Park Ave., New York, NY (U.S.) 10021.

Darling, Martha. *The Role of Women in the Economy: Summary of Ten National Reports* (1975). Organisation for Economic Cooperation and Development, 2 Rue André Pascal, FO 75775, Paris (France) CEDEX 16.

Eastham, Kay. "Women on the Move: Affirmative Action for Women Crown Employees in Ontario." *The Canadian Business Review*, III, No. 2 (1976), 34–35.

Education Development Center. *Business as Usual: Sex Stereotyping in Business Education* (undated). WEEA Distribution Center, 55 Chapel St., Newton, MA (U.S.) 02160.

Employers Council of British Columbia. *Female Employment in Nontraditional Areas: Some Attitudes of Managers and Working Women* (1975). 800 W. Pender, Vancouver, British Columbia (Canada) V6C 2V6.

Frank, Harold H. *Women in the Organization* (1977). University of Pennsylvania Press, 3933 Walnut St., Philadelphia, PA (U.S.) 19104

Graham, Alma. *Non-Sexist Language Guidelines* (1975). Dictionary Division, American Heritage Publishing Company, 1221 Avenue of the Americas, New York, NY (U.S.) 10020.

Henley, Nancy, and Barrie Thorne. *She Said, He*

Said (1975). KNOW, Inc., P.O. Box 86031, Pittsburgh, PA (U.S.) 15221.

Hogan, Patricia. "Sexism in the Corporate Press." *Journal of Organizational Communication* (U.S.), II (Winter, 1973), 1–6.

International Institute for Labour Studies. *Women and Decision-Making: A Social Priority* (November, 1975). 4 Route Des Morillons, CH-1211 Genève 22, Switzerland.

John Wiley & Sons. *Wiley Guidelines on Sexism in Language* (1977). 605 Third Ave., New York, NY (U.S.) 10158.

Lakoff, Robin. *Language and Women's Place,* Harper Colophon 398 (1975). Harper & Row, 10 E. 53rd St., New York, NY (U.S.) 10022.

McGraw-Hill Book Company. *Guidelines for Equal Treatment of the Sexes in McGraw-Hill Book Company Publications* (1974). 1211 Avenue of the Americas, New York, NY (U.S.) 10020.

Miller, Casey, and Kate Swift. *Handbook for Nonsexist Writing for Writers, Editors and Speakers* (1980). Lippincott & Crowell, 531 Fifth Ave., New York, NY (U.S.) 10017, or Fitzhenry and Whiteside Ltd., 150 Les Mills Road, Don Mills, Toronto, Ontario (Canada) M3B 2T5.

Words and Women: New Language in New Times (1976). Anchor Press/Doubleday, 501 Franklin Ave., Garden City, Long Island, NY (U.S.) 11530.

Moore, Joy, and Frank Laverty. "Positive Action for Integrating Women Into Management." *Canadian Personnel and Industrial Relations Journal,* XXII, No. 2 (1975), 15–21.

Morris, William, and Mary Morris. *Harper*

Dictionary of Contemporary Usage (1975). Harper & Row, 10 E. 53rd St., New York, NY (U.S.) 10022.
National Council of Teachers of English. *Guidelines for Nonsexist Use of Language in NCTE Publications* (1975). 1111 Kenyon Road, Urbana, IL (U.S.) 61801.

Sexism and Language (1977). Address above.
O'Neil, William. *Women at Work* (1972). Quadrangle Books, 330 Madison Ave., New York, NY (U.S.) 10017.
Ontario Educational Communications Authority. *Video Resource Catalogue on Women's Studies* (1979). Central Order Desk, Box 200, Station Q, Toronto, Ontario (Canada) M4T 2T1.
"Sexual Harassment Lands Companies in Court." *Business Week* (U.S.), October 1, 1979, pp. 120–22.
Stead, Bette Ann. *Women in Management* (1978). Prentice-Hall, Englewood Cliffs, NJ (U.S.) 07632.
Stevens, Betsy. "Improving Communication With Clerical Workers: The Non-Sexist Directive." *Personnel Journal* (U.S.), LVI, No. 4 (1977), 170–172.
Tatner, Ronnie Steinberg. *Equal Employment Policy for Women: Strategies for Implementation in the U.S., Canada and Western Europe* (1980). Temple University Press, Broad and Oxford, Philadelphia, PA (U.S.) 19122.
"The American Woman: On the Move—But Where?" *U.S. News and World Report*, December 8, 1975, p. 54.
Vick, Judy. "Sexual Harassment—Can It Be Stopped?" *Corporate Report* (U.S.), X, No. 10 (1979), 33–34.

"Words That Make Women Disappear." *Redbook* (U.S.), March, 1977, p. 72.

Zuker, Marvin A., and June Callwood. *The Law Is Not for Women* (1976). Pitman Publishing, 517 Wellington W., Toronto, Ontario (Canada) M5V 1G1.

Age

Children's Express. *Listen to Us!* (1978). Workman Publishing Company, One W. 39th St., New York, NY (U.S.) 10018.

National Gray Panthers Media Watch. Complaint center for media bias against older persons. 475 Riverside Dr., Room 861, New York, NY (U.S.) 10115.

Older Women's League. Established to educate the public on the needs of older women. 3800 Harrison St., Oakland, CA (U.S.) 94611.

Spencer, Mary E. *Truth About Aging: Guidelines for Publishers* (1979). National Retired Teachers Association and American Association of Retired Persons, 1909 K St., N.W., Washington, DC (U.S.) 20049.

Disability

Bowe, Frank. *Handicapping America: Barriers to Disabled People* (1978). Harper & Row, 10 E. 53rd St., New York, NY (U.S.) 10022.

Bruck, Lilly. *Access: The Guide to a Better Life for Disabled America* (1978). Random House, 201 E. 50th St., New York, NY (U.S.) 10022.

Council for Exceptional Children. *Guidelines for the Representation of Exceptional Persons in Education Material* (1977). 1920 Association Dr., Reston, VA (U.S.) 22091.

Fleishman, Edwin A. "Evaluating Physical Abilities Required for Jobs." *Personnel Administrator* (U.S.), XXIV (June, 1979), 82–92.

Helen Keller International, Incorporated. Established to improve the quality of life for disabled (especially blind) persons. Supports research and can provide a variety of information; also publishes a newsletter. 22 W. 17th St., New York, NY (U.S.) 10011.

McGraw-Hill Book Company. *Guidelines for Fair Representation of Disabled People in McGraw-Hill Book Company Publications* (1980). 1211 Avenue of the Americas, New York, NY (U.S.) 10020.

Milk, Leslie B. "The Key to Job Accommodations." *Personnel Administrator* (U.S.), XXIV (January, 1979), 31–33, 38.

Rappaport, Cyril M. "Hiring the Handicapped." *Personnel Administrator* (U.S.), XXV (November, 1980), 81–88.

U.N. Council for the International Year of Disabled Persons. In addition to ongoing programs, this United Nations-established council has special materials prepared for the International Year of Disabled Persons (1981). 1575 Eye St., N.W., Suite 430, Washington, DC (U.S.) 20005.

Yoder, Dale, and Hubert G. Heneman, Jr. *ASPA Handbook of Personnel and Industrial Relations* (1979). Bureau of National Affairs, Inc., 1231 25th St., N.W., Washington, DC (U.S.) 20037.

Biographies

Stewart L. Burge, ABC, is Manager of Communication Programs for GTE Automatic Electric, Inc., Chicago. A frequent lecturer and workshop leader on audiovisual communication, he has written articles on AV production for communication and training journals. Accredited by IABC, he received degrees in journalism and broadcast communication from West Virginia University.

Clara Degen is Director of Research for the International Association of Business Communicators in San Francisco. A journalism graduate of Indiana University, she has been both journalist and public-relations practitioner, as well as the coauthor of four books on fund-raising and on music education.

Lucille DeView is an award-winning journalist and freelance writer in Kalkaska, Michigan, and, until recently, was director of the writers' training program at *The Christian Science Monitor*. She has taught college-level journalism and continues to lead writing seminars. She is author of *Up North, A Contemporary Woman's Walden* (Indian Village Press).

Loisanne M. Foerster, ABC, is Director of Foerst Place, a business communication consulting firm based in Crozet, Virginia. As past coordinator of IABC's Committee on Women in Business Communication, she conceived the idea for this guidebook and developed the original manuscript on sexism. She has an undergraduate degree in communication management from Park College and a graduate degree in liberal arts from Southern Methodist University.

Myra L. Kruger is Manager of Employee Communication for 3M Company in St. Paul. She formerly headed IABC's Chapter Advisory Committee and its Special Interest Committee. She earned her undergraduate degree in English from South Dakota State University.

Catherine M. Meek is a principal in the Los Angeles office of Towers, Perrin, Forster & Crosby. She holds a graduate degree from the University of Glasgow and was a contributing author to *The Manager's Guide to Equal Employment Opportunity* and *EEO Today* (both Executive Enterprises) and to *Personnel Management: Compensation Service* (Prentice-Hall).

Marianne Glofcheski Ménard is Coordinator of Equal Opportunities at Algonquin College, Ottawa. She is also an adult educator, learning facilitator, and community educator at the school, as well as a member of its executive committee on continuing education. Her graduate degree in education is from the University of Ottawa.

Mary Munter is Director of the Communication Skills Program at the Stanford Graduate School of Business, Stanford. In addition, she consults with and provides executive training for corporations and nonprofit groups. She earned her degrees in English from Stanford and is author of *A Concise Guide to Managerial Communication* (Prentice-Hall).

Judy E. Pickens, ABC, is a communication consultant in Seattle. She was chief editor on the first edition of this book, as well as the author of the chapters on disability and visuals. Accredited by IABC, she received her graduate degree in journalism from Kansas State University and is author of *The Freelancer's Handbook: A Comprehensive Guide to Selling Your Freelance Services* (Prentice-Hall).

Lester R. Potter, ABC, is Director of the Personnel Division of MFC Services in Madison, Mississippi. An accredited member of IABC, he has served on the association's executive and district boards and has completed numerous committee and special assignments. He received his degree in communication from the University of Southern Mississippi.

Linda Cook Roberts is Director of Communication for Hay Associates in San Francisco. A winner of IABC's Gold Quill for her affirmative-action communication program while with Bank of America, she is an English and journalism graduate of the University of Michigan and received her graduate degree in organizational development from Pepperdine University.

Index